WOOD ARCHITECTURE

LAURENCE KING

First published in Great Britain in 2005

This paperback edition published in 2009
by Laurence King Publishing Ltd
361–373 City Road
London EC1V 1LR
T + 44 (0)20 7841 6900
F + 44 (0)20 7841 6910
E enquiries@laurenceking.co.uk
www.laurenceking.co.uk

Text © 2005 Ruth Slavid

A catalogue record for this book is
available from the British Library

ISBN 978 1 85669 606 7

Designed by Mark Vernon-Jones
Cover design by FL@33
Cover images by ©Bill Noll/
iStockphoto.com (top);©Selahattin
Bayram/iStockphoto.com (bottom left);
iStockphoto.com (bottom right)

Printed in China

WOOD ARCHITECTURE

RUTH SLAVID

Laurence King Publishing

CONTENTS

OPPOSITE
At Peckham Library in South London, Alsop Architects have used curved ply cladding on the self-contained 'pods' and on other elements, such as the main desk.

BELOW
The embodied energy involved in the production of one tonne of timber is less than that for an equivalent weight of the other major construction materials. (Source: Forest and Wood Products Research and Development Corp., Australia.)

RIGHT
Managed forests, like this one in Washington State, are the most effective and environmentally responsible method of producing timber for construction.

Is timber a contemporary material? The projects in this book show that the answer must be a resounding yes, but it is a question that would have received a much more tentative answer only a couple of decades ago. Steeped in tradition – the oldest known timber buildings are log houses found in Poland, dating from about 700 BC – timber is a material that has scarcely seemed at the forefront of technology in recent times.

The heroic age of the Industrial Revolution was concerned with showing how structures could be made larger than ever before. As the potential of cast iron, and, later, of steel, came to be understood better, and as reinforced concrete was developed, timber seemed like the poor relation – the traditional material that was all right for a vernacular building, cheap housing or a small footbridge, but was not a player in the big league.

Two factors have led to change. One is the advance of the environmental movement and a concomitant growth

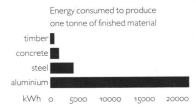

Energy consumed to produce one tonne of finished material

timber	
concrete	
steel	
aluminium	

kWh 0   5000   10000   15000   20000

of interest in traditional methods of construction. Timber is a renewable material and, given sustainable forestry techniques, an environmentally acceptable one. Wood absorbs carbon dioxide as it grows, and the gas remains locked up during the wood's lifespan in a building and during any subsequent reuse. It also scores well in terms of 'embodied' energy, the amount of energy needed to produce a unit of timber, compared to other structural materials. For example, it takes 750MJ of energy to create a cubic metre (35 cubic feet) of rough-sawn timber, compared to 266,000MJ for a cubic metre of steel and 1,100, 000MJ for a cubic metre of aluminium. Timber is, of course, less dense than the other materials, but make the comparison on weight and it is still impressive: 1.5MJ per kilogram (2¼ pounds) of rough-sawn timber, 35MJ per kilogram of steel and 435MJ per kilogram of aluminium.

At the same time, timber has become much more engineered than it used to be, with the development of glue-laminated material, the understanding of stressed-skin structures, and the ability to use almost every part of a tree, including the sweepings that go into chipboard. This is partly a measure of the ingenuity of manufacturers, encouraged by imaginative architects and engineers, and partly a response to changing circumstances.

A DIFFERENT MATERIAL

Timber is not the same as it once was. Just as the agricultural revolution changed the nature of crops and farm animals – so that, although the word 'pig' was commonly understood in the Middle Ages and is so today, the animal has changed out of all recognition in the intervening centuries – so timber has altered as well. Originally, timber came from virgin forest, a practice that did not end until Asia and South America were persuaded to stop depleting their resources in a way that Europe had done centuries earlier. Nearly all timber now comes from managed second- or third-growth forest. Silviculture is a complex discipline, which attempts to balance productivity with environmental concerns, ranging from the preservation of natural fauna to the protection of watercourses, but there is always pressure for relatively rapid commercial returns.

In America, for example, it was believed until the 1920s that only old-growth timber from virgin forest was suitable for structural use. Increased understanding of the way that timber grows and should be cut means that this is no longer the case. But using secondary growth means that there will be a lot more juvenile timber. In most cases, timber from trees less than about 30 years old is considerably softer than that from mature trees. It is also smaller, adding to the cost of large structural elements or even of the kind of wide floorboards that were common in houses until the end of the nineteenth century. Another consideration is that production is seasonal. This may not be immediately apparent if you are buying standard timber harvested and stored in large quantities. But manufacturers of specialist veneers, for example, find that architects show little appreciation of the fact that all harvesting takes place during the dormant period in autumn, and that, by the following summer, stocks may be running low.

One solution to these problems is to use specialist cutting and grading, which ensures that architects get exactly what they want, but manufactured products come much closer than 'raw' timber to offering the consistency of properties found in steel and concrete, while offering the moral satisfaction of cutting down on waste. However, the environmental purist is likely to be concerned about the nature of the glues and resins that bind these products, and there are implications for recycling.

STICKING TOGETHER

Of all engineered solutions, probably the most influential is 'glulam', short for glued laminated timber. This is a structural timber product manufactured

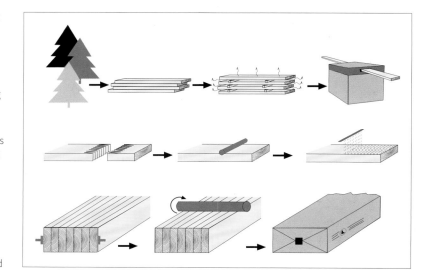

by gluing together individual flat pieces of wood under controlled conditions. The timber laminates are strength-graded before fabrication. The member can be straight or curved, and can be made with a variable section to satisfy structural requirements.

Early structures built using glue-laminated timber included a lantern roof, with laminated, curved support beams, at the Old Rusholme Chapel in Manchester (1827), which survived until it was demolished in 1962, and the assembly hall of King Edward College in Southampton (1860), but these projects were rarities. The technology derived from earlier work in Germany, where Carl Friedrich von Wiebeking had used

laminated timber in the construction of road bridges. The normal technique for securing those elements was with bolts, although on a bridge at Altenmarkt the laminates were glued.

The French developed the idea of using curved laminated timbers, with Armand Rose Emy applying his ideas to a roof of horizontally laminated timber arches in a trial at Marac, near Bayonne, in 1825. But this was something of a false dawn. The development of wrought iron in 1850 squeezed out the need for large-span timber structures, which, in any case, experienced problems with rot and with the glues that were used. The next growth in importance of glulam occurred when Otto Hetzer, a scientist

LEFT
One of the earliest uses of glulam in the UK was on the Waterloo entrance arches built for the Festival of Britain in 1951, and subsequently demolished.

BELOW
Architects Pringle Richards Sharratt created parabolic arches, reminiscent of the Waterloo entrance, for their Sheffield Winter Gardens, completed in 2002.

by Pringle Richards Sharratt. This building has structural arches shaped as parabolas, so that the line of action of the forces lies within the arches when they carry the building's self-weight. The laminates are made from larch, which is relatively hard, minimizing minor damage where it is exposed in the public space, and durable enough to last for a long time if it is detailed to ensure that it does not remain wet. Sheffield Winter Gardens is an example of a project where glulam not only supplies a structurally intelligent solution, but also forms one of the main visual elements of the project. It is a harmonious solution for a space populated by plants.

OTHER ENGINEERED FORMS

A newer type of parallel laminate product is known as laminated veneer lumber (LVL). Thin sheets of wood are peeled from the log (in a similar manner to, but more thickly than, the veneers used in making plywood) and cut into shorter lengths, which are overlapped and glued together to provide the required thickness, and then cut into structural-sized sections. With all the grains running parallel, LVL has the same directional properties as sawn timber, but is more uniform. It is possible to make unjointed lengths of up to 26 metres (85 feet) in this way. Although it may be stronger than glulam, LVL is

at a factory in Weimar, registered a patent in 1906 for glulam structures using casein glue. Casein, which is derived from cows' milk, is not moisture-resistant, however, and the real success of glulam depended on the development of modern glues, such as resorcinol and melamine formaldehyde, which resist both water and heat.

In the UK, for example, the use of glulam dates back to the Festival of Britain in 1951, when it was used for the parabolic entrance arches. In the 1950s, shapes that became fashionable, such as conoids and hyperbolic paraboloids, were built of glulam. The material tended to be used in such buildings as churches, where its aesthetic seemed

appropriate, or in swimming pools and ice-hockey stadiums, where the humid atmosphere could be inimical to structural steel and to the reinforcing steel in concrete.

In the 1970s, glulam became more of a commodity material, as techniques for producing curved beams improved, and high-volume plants were built in many northern European countries to produce straight beams in a wide choice of standard section sizes. As a result, consumption of glulam in the UK doubled between 1985 and 1995.

Recent projects making exemplary use of glulam include the Sheffield Winter Gardens in northern England, designed

BELOW
Plywood is made by
'peeling' thin layers of
logs and laying each
resulting veneer at
right angles to its
neighbours.

commonly seen as a less attractive material, and is therefore less likely to be used as a central architectural feature.

LVL was used by British architect Studio E, with engineer Techniker, to create the panels on a curved pod for an experimental educational building in London. Shigeru Ban used it to create a children's nursery in Odate, Japan, (see page 172), but on his Atsushi Imai Memorial Gymnasium in the same town (page 180) he used laminated strand lumber (LSL). Another material made from veneer sheets is parallel strand lumber (PSL). The sheets are cut into small strips, dried and, after spraying

with adhesive, formed into a billet, which is dried again. This allows the formation of strong, relatively deep structural members that can be used for beams or columns.

BOARD GAMES
There is a wide variety of boards available for cladding, flooring and other applications. Midway between a board and a structural element is laminated strand lumber (LSL), which can be up to 120 cm (48 inches) long, up to 19 cm (8 inches) wide and 13 cm (5 inches) deep. It is made by cutting logs into short 'bolts' that go through a rotary slicer, making them into strands about 30 cm (11 inches) long. The dried strands are formed into a mat, so that they are parallel to each other, and the mat is bound with adhesive, pressed and dried, before being cut into smaller units.

The best-known board is plywood, a product so common that one tends not to think about how it is made. (Its origins are very old. The sarcophagi of Egyptian mummies were made from a form of plywood.) In fact, the manufacturing method is fascinating and far more closely controlled than might be imagined. Plywood is made by a veneer process, meaning that it is made from peeling a log, but the veneers are much thinner than in the manufacture of LVL.

Modern production began with the introduction of the first veneer lathes in the USA in the mid-nineteenth century.

To make plywood, the veneers are laid so that the grain of each layer is at right angles to that of the layer below, and the two outermost layers are placed in such a way that their grains run in the same direction. A special resin adhesive is used to bond the boards, which are then pressed together under heat. After drying, they are trimmed, then surface defects, such as knotholes, are repaired and the plywood is sanded. Different grades of plywood are determined by the quality of the surface. Birch-faced

plywood – available from Finland, Russia and Latvia – also comes in various grades, determined by whether birch veneers are also used for the internal layers. The more birch there is, the stronger the material will be. Whether or not a plywood is suitable to be used externally depends largely on the glue that has been used in its construction.

(Phenol formaldehyde is fine out of doors, but urea formaldehyde is not.)

The toughest of all plywoods is marine plywood, made from durable hardwoods. Many architects specify marine plywood when it is not really necessary. As a result, there are two types of marine plywood. The type aimed specifically at the construction industry is not, despite its name, deemed suitable for marine use.

Plywood is defined as a layered composite, but there are also more complex kinds, with names such as blockboard and laminboard, which have timber-strip cores and a stiffer surface, often of plywood. These composites offer a way of using lower-quality elements at the centre of a board, while achieving good qualities and attractive properties.

Particle composites come in three categories: particleboards, oriented strand boards and structural particleboard. Particleboards can be of wood chipboard, flaxboard or cement-bonded particleboard. Chipboard, a common and inexpensive material, is made by breaking up wood mechanically into particles, which are graded, dried, blended with glue and formed into mats. The mats are pressed at high temperature and dried to provide a panel that can be trimmed

RIGHT
The McDonald's
headquarters in
Helsinki, Finland,
designed by
Heikkinen-Komonen
Architects and
completed in 1997,

was one of the first
buildings to be clad
in Thermowood,
softwood that
becomes harder
and more durable
as a result of heat
treatment.

and sanded to size. Again, there are a number of grades available, distingushed by the particle size and the glue used.

Flaxboard is not a timber product at all. It uses flax waste, rather than wood particles, and has a lower specification than the other particleboards. Cement-bonded particleboard uses cement, rather than glue, to bind wood particles, which form only 20 to 30 per cent by weight of the total. It is about twice as dense as plywood, but offers advantages in wet conditions, in a fire or when under fungal or insect attack. It also has good sound absorbency.

Oriented strand boards are intended for external use. They are similar in both price and performance to softwood ply. Softwood strands, at least twice as long as they are thick, are used to make the boards. The strands are in three layers, with those in the top and bottom layers oriented roughly parallel to the length of the board and those in the middle layer at right angles. Exterior-grade phenolic resins are used as a binder.

Fibreboards also come in a variety of forms. The best-known are hardboard and MDF (medium density fibreboard), the latter beloved of the makers of inexpensive furniture and participants in television makeover shows. All the boards mix wood fibres with a binder, by either a wet or a dry process. MDF is

made by a dry process that gives it a very smooth finish. It is fairly dense, although it will creep under load with time; and, although it is easily cut, the process produces large quantities of dust.

HARD TIMES

Composite materials make it possible to get more out of relatively low-grade timber. Another approach is to improve the properties of the timber itself, enabling the use of relatively inexpensive softwoods where, previously, hardwoods would have been specified. There are two main techniques, one that 'cooks' the timber and another that impregnates it with a binder. Both tackle the weak points of timber – susceptibility to rotting and lack of dimensional stability – as well as improving its mechanical properties.

Water is the enemy of timber. Damp wood is susceptible to attack by fungi and insects. In addition, timber will swell when damp and shrink when it dries out, a cycle that can lead to cracking or to problems with adjacent materials. The rule of thumb is that hardwoods perform better than softwoods, and that some very dense (and very expensive) hardwoods perform very well indeed. In many applications, the solution has been to use softwoods treated with a preservative. The most commonly used preservative is copper chrome arsenate (CCA), which, although highly effective, is

toxic to wildlife, and the ingredients are unpleasant for humans, too. Many people argue that, used properly, CCA is perfectly safe, but even its proponents agree that waste timber treated with CCA should not be used for domestic fires or barbecues. Concern about CCA arose particularly because of its widespread use on playground equipment, and some countries, including Germany and Austria, have placed severe restrictions on its use.

Environmentalists see boron as the most acceptable alternative to CCA. But a treatment introduced by Finnish company FinnForest actually removes the need for chemicals. Called Thermowood, it involves heating timber

for up to 25 hours at a temperature of 190–240°C (375–475°F) in an oxygen-free environment, so that it doesn't catch fire. During heating, the moisture content drops dramatically and the wood undergoes an irreversible change, becoming harder, more stable and darker in colour, with a moisture content of only about 8 per cent. There is a similar process available in France, and one in the Netherlands called PLATO. The only disadvantage, apart from the energy used in heating, is that the bending strength of the wood reduces slightly and it becomes more brittle. This can make fixing difficult unless, for example, holes are pre-drilled. Pioneered in Finland, and first used on such projects as the McDonald's headquarters in Helsinki, Thermowood has been specified on a number of residential projects in Denmark. In the UK, one of its first commercial uses was on the Beehive shopping centre in Cambridge, designed by Benoy.

The alternative is a process offered by Indurite, a company founded in New Zealand but now based in London, which involves impregnating timber with a starch-based, non-toxic food derivative and then drying it at relatively low temperatures. The starch reacts with the timber, increasing its hardness. Dyes can also be included in the process, changing the colour of the wood. According to Indurite, durability and dimensional stability improve greatly. Originally used on New Zealand softwoods, the process is now being extended to other timbers. The Building Research Establishment in England has been awarded a grant from the Forestry Commission and Scottish Enterprise to evaluate the performance of the Indurite treatment on UK plantation species. Indurite also has an office in Seattle, Washington, from where it is exploring the possibility of introducing the process to the USA. Until now, the focus has been on flooring and some specially designed furniture, but this may be extended to cladding.

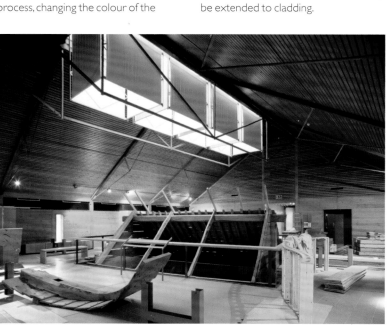

BETTER BY DESIGN

Improved design has made it possible for softwoods to be used in applications not previously considered appropriate. Architect Chris Wilderspin of van Heyningen & Haward, who has worked on a number of buildings that use softwood cladding, advocates the use of preservatives, but likes them to be environmentally non-aggressive. 'My practice's timber-clad buildings, such as the Sutton Hoo visitor centre in Suffolk, and the Gateway to the White Cliffs visitor centre in Dover, benefit from generous roof overhangs and proper plinths to lift the cladding away from the ground,' says Wilderspin. Softwood cladding should be used as a rainscreen, he argues, with adequate ventilation behind it. Even with good protection, there will be some weather-induced changes to dimensions, which the design must accommodate.

WASTE NOT

It is environmentally desirable to keep waste to a minimum. Although lower-grade timber can be used in items such as particleboards, it would be marvellous if the material could find more direct applications. This was the thinking behind the work of architects Ahrends Burton and Koralek, and Edward Cullinan Architects, at Hooke Park, a furniture-making college in England. Working with engineer Buro Happold on a number of projects, they developed ways of building structures with unseasoned roundwood, the timber from the small trees thinned out from a plantation. Although the aesthetic is slightly folksy, the engineering is not. For example, the professionals developed new steel joints for the timber that would accommodate both its mechanical properties and the shrinkage that would occur as it aged.

A research project funded by the European Community on the use of roundwood concluded that its main application was likely to be in rural areas, particularly for holiday and leisure use, in buildings such as cottages and footbridges. Austria and Finland, in particular, were identified as potential markets. In Finland, for example, 1.8 million cubic metres (64 million cubic feet) of roundwood of 8 to 15 cm (3 to 6 inches) in diameter are produced every year. At present, most of this is used for paper-industry pulp or firewood. Part of the task, the researchers acknowledge, is changing attitudes, but they are also tackling such issues as harvesting, jointing and structural details. Purdue University in Indiana is also carrying out research on the topic, producing prototype frames and details, as well as recommending that the material could find uses in furniture for schools.

GOING GREEN

Another way of reducing the amount of intervention is to use a material such as 'green' oak for either framing or cladding. Green oak is oak that has been stored for 12 to 18 months, allowing it to lose the tensions set up by the felling process. The timber still has a high moisture content, which makes it easier to work than seasoned timber, but the architect must take account of the shrinkage that will occur over the first few years of the building's life.

DEALING WITH STRESS

The processes described above concern the use of timber that is as near to its natural state as possible. But it is equally valid to push the properties of timber to the limit, either by sophisticated engineering or by pairing it with other materials. This extends its performance, allowing it to replace another material or saving on total material quantities, or both.

One common approach is to use stressed-skin panels, composite members in which the framing and the sheet materials are designed to act together for greater efficiency. It was first developed for aeroplane construction, on such planes as de Havilland's Mosquito in the Second World War and Howard Hughes's doomed giant, the Spruce Goose, in 1947. As with glulam, the technique was dependent on the availability of a new generation of glues, with high-strength options based on

BELOW LEFT
Canadian architect
Bing Thom used
stressed-skin
construction for the
roof of the Lo
Residence in
Vancouver, Canada.

BELOW
Konrad Frey used
stressed-skin ply in
box sections for a roof
that spans 16 metres
(52 feet) on his
prototype solar-
production building at
Hartberg in Austria.

resorcinol formaldehyde replacing the
traditional casein glues. From
aeroplanes, the technology migrated to
floors and, later, to buildings. American
architect Bruce Goff was one of the first
to recognize its potential. Working with
engineer J. Palmer Boggs, he designed
undercut walls and coffin-shaped
profiles of stressed-skin plywood in the
geometrically extraordinary house he
created for his patron, Joe Price, in 1956.
Some recent examples of the technique
include elegantly understated buildings
for the Ecopark in Hartberg, Austria, by
Konrad Frey, and the much more
exuberant stressed-skin roof of the Lo
Residence in Vancouver, by Canadian
architect Bing Thom, which combines
plywood with zinc cladding.

ON A PLATE
Another flexible technique involves the
use of lamellar roofs, where a number of
small regular elements are built up to
form a plate that acts structurally in a
continuous way. It makes possible a
building of great technical efficiency and
often of considerable beauty. The
technique has been used successfully
at Hounslow East station in London
(see page 118) and also at an office
headquarters in southern England,
where Anglo-American architect
Gensler created four gridshell roofs
that define the form of the buildings.

As with all truly three-dimensional
modern design processes, the successful
and efficient execution of such

BELOW LEFT AND
BELOW
Gensler designed four
gridshell roofs for this
financial services
headquarters in
southern England.

structures depends on sophisticated computer design techniques, as well as on the imagination of architects and the clear thinking of engineers. Already, it is possible to perform routinely calculations that once would have been impossible. As computing power continues to improve, we should see an increasing and increasingly sophisticated number of these natural-seeming forms.

MIX AND MATCH

Now that timber is no longer the preserve of the purist, imaginative designers often use it in combination with another material, most often steel, to take advantage of the properties of both. At the Swiss pavilion for Expo 2000 in Hanover, for example (see page 56), Peter Zumthor used steel tension rods to give stability to the stacks of unseasoned timber that formed the walls.

Another approach is to use flitched timber, where steel plates are sandwiched between timber elements. The steel element provides strength and rigidity, with the thicker timber elements preventing buckling of the steel plate. In this way, the structure makes very efficient use of both elements. Sharples Holden and Pasquarelli, working with engineer Buro Happold, used this technique on the house for a carousel at Greenport Village, New York (page 196), in order to make the structure as slender as possible.

It is also possible to make composite beams by combining different types of timber products. Typically, a webbed beam will use solid timber or structural timber composites for the top and bottom flanges, and plywood or other board material, such as oriented strand board, for the web. The flanges resist the tensile and compressive forces, and the web resists the shear.

HOW DOES IT LOOK?

Given the wealth of ways in which timber can be used, is wood architecture moving in a particular aesthetic direction? The simple answer is no. As more architects embrace the use of timber, so the diversity of ways in which it is used increases.

Some architects take a deliberately traditional approach. You will have no difficulty in buying an off-the-peg log cabin if that is what you want, a traditional structure that comes complete with electric sockets, sewage outlets and doubtless a place to position a satellite dish. This sort of lowest-common-denominator architecture is often far less offensive than a lot of the speculative housing that goes up in brick and block, or in concrete and render.

But even the log cabin has been embraced as an idea that can be brought up to date. On the outskirts of Moscow, the traditional *dacha*, or wooden chalet, has been recreated on a Brobdingnagian scale to contain a

treasure-house of historic fittings and furnishings for sale, known simply as 'Dacha'. More radically, Moscow practices Savinkin/Kuz'min and First Architectural Studio/ARP Studio have designed out-of-town homes that use stacked logs as a major element, but juxtapose them with concrete and steel. There is something shocking about the modernist cliché of a bright-blue swimming pool crossed by a steel and glass bridge when it sits in a log building.

Russia, which has more forest than any other country, also has a tradition of workmen skilled with axes, capable of adapting any element in situ to make it fit. This craft approach still survives in many countries and is used on the most

surprising buildings, for instance on Foster's Chesa Futura building in Switzerland (see page 70), where the international high priest of high-tech has used local craftsmen to cut larch shingles in a traditional manner. Such pragmatism was probably behind the decision of a trio of young London-based architects, Silvia Ullmayer, Annalie Riches and Barti Garibaldo, to choose engineered timber as the structural material when they experimented with the concept of designing, and partly constructing themselves, three linked houses for their own occupation.

TRANSGRESSING TRADITION
Some of the projects in this book are the opposite of pragmatic. Architects

and engineers have pushed timber to its limits to create tours de force of structural engineering, elegant structures that also leave observers muttering, 'I didn't realize you could do that.' Yet there is a kind of transgression here. Yes, timber can perform magnificently and be used in more slender forms than anybody once imagined; it can span great distances and adopt graceful curves; it can be designed so that the traditional enemies of fire and damp and rot are virtually banished. Timber, so often associated with tradition, with the vernacular, can be a thoroughly modern material.

It can, but it isn't exactly easy. One architect has calculated that there is a

substantial cost premium in choosing to use wood rather than steel or concrete, simply because of the extra work required by the designer. Steel and concrete are the materials that evolved to satisfy the ambitions of today's ever more demanding designers – and they still have the edge. We can now construct six-storey buildings in timber, but we will never see a 40-storey skyscraper with a timber frame. There are some magnificent timber footbridges, but we will never see a timber suspension bridge carrying six lanes of traffic over a river estuary. Timber may work well as a material for railway stations, but it will not be used to form the tunnels that carry those railway lines underground.

and pushing the boundaries sets up an opposition to that idea, a tension that balances tradition with invention and makes timber one of the most exciting and modern materials with which to work.

British architect Bernard Stilwell admits that he used timber as a Trojan horse when he designed a library building in March, Cambridgeshire. 'If we are doing some fairly serious architectural things with severe geometry,' he says, 'timber avoids people's feeling that the shape is too harsh, and hence trying to soften it up. It is something they can empathize with.'

By that definition, some of the buildings in this book are also Trojan horses. And all of them are surprising. Each is an ambitious building in its own way, and because it marries ambition with a material that people know through historical association and everyday familiarity, it confounds the users' expectations. The best timber buildings convey a sense of newness and unfamiliarity, while remaining almost incapable of being ugly or alienating. That is what unites the buildings in this book, whether grown in place from a group of trees or engineered with the most advanced CAD tools available.

At its limits, timber will never be able to do what steel and concrete can do. All the efforts of designers, all the clever calculations, the manufacturing technology and the tight tolerances of construction can only help to bring it closer to the performance of rival materials. It will never surpass them. So why bother?

WARM FEELINGS

For some (probably most) architects working with timber, part of the justification for its use is environmental. But there is also the issue of appearance. Timber is warm, non-threatening, tactile. Even the grey to which exposed cedar weathers is a warmer grey than the grey-white of concrete or the blue-white of untreated steel. In all buildings that use timber, with the strange exception of the timber-framed house in places with a tradition of masonry construction, you see the timber that is used in the building. It gives a human scale; it is a material that most people feel happy with, which they like to touch and, often, smell.

Architects designing in steel and concrete can fall into the trap of making a building seem too impersonal, too machine-like, too large and cold. With timber, the danger is the opposite — a building can seem overcrafted, too *heimlich*, too folksy. But an architect who starts playing with technology

OPPOSITE
When Olavi Koponen designed a summer house in Finland, it was on an island so remote that not only did it have to be constructed by hand, many materials were also delivered by horse and cart.

What could be more natural than a timber building? Despite the engineering expertise, the careful fabrication, the timber treatments, the glues that hold manufactured timber together, wood is still acknowledged and valued as a natural material. For those who want to build in beautiful spots, it seems, dare one say, the natural choice.

It certainly was for Steven Holl when he designed the Y House in the Catskill mountains of New York State, and for Cutler Anderson with the Reeve Residence on Lopez Island off the coast of Seattle (see pages 40 and 44). Both these houses occupy lovely sites and are oriented to make the most of stunning views. Australian architects, such as Sean Godsell and Ken Latona, have followed the same strategy, establishing what seems to be a new national tradition; timber has also been used in such projects as Brian MacKay-Lyons's Danielson House in Nova Scotia, Canada.

The examples mentioned are all relatively large houses that offer the opportunity of gracious living, but there is another approach that harks back to the idea of a simple wooden hut. If you want to get away from it all – and many new timber houses tend to be weekend homes, rather than full-time residences – then surely it would be nice to divest

yourself of a lot of the paraphernalia of everyday life. Roberto Briccola's simple, but sophisticated, wooden refuge in Switzerland draws on the history of wooden chalets and log cabins in northern Europe (see page 24). In Denmark, Henning Larsen has created an artist's house in Zealand of similarly breathtaking simplicity; in Finland, Olavi Koponen has designed a house on an island that was not only built by hand, but also had many of its materials delivered by horse and cart. Nor does this philosophy need to be restricted to one-off buildings for the well-heeled. At Paintrock Camp in Wyoming, Charles Rose Architects have designed an education centre for city children, dedicated to ensuring that they are as close as possible to nature (see page 34). The project elevates them above the ground on a series of timber platforms and lets them sleep in buildings that can open up to the natural surroundings as much as the weather allows.

Being in touch with nature involves more than lovely views and minimal visual intrusion on the landscape. Another issue is using wood in a way that responds to how trees grow. At the Weald and Downland Museum in southern England, Edward Cullinan Architects have collaborated with one of the most advanced engineering practices to use green oak (that is, oak

that has not been dried) to construct a gridshell and clad it in locally sourced timber (see page 28). This follows earlier projects that made extensive use not just of green oak, but also of timber thinnings, trees usually discarded as part of the cultivation process.

Such projects incorporate timber that has received minimal treatment after being cut down. But the real purist may ask why it is necessary to cut down trees at all. For example, in Germany, Marcel Kalberer has brought a strong architectural sensibility to a project that otherwise might seem to be on the lunatic fringe: training trees to grow into 'living' structures (see page 20). Although hardly likely to become a mainstream design method – shelter is incomplete and seasonal – Kalberer's work demonstrates that it is possible to adopt an extremely fundamental approach to the use of timber and still create something beautiful.

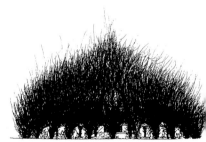

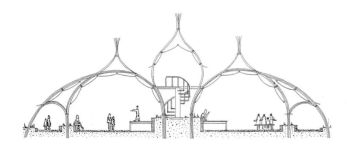

OPPOSITE
TOP   Marcel Kalberer visualized the way that the Auerworld palace would evolve through growth, from shortly after completion in 1998 (far left) up until 2012 (far right).
BOTTOM   Leaves are starting to obscure the structure in summer.

THIS PAGE
TOP   Section through the Auerworld palace.
TOP RIGHT   The flexibility of willow whips allows them to adopt the architect's chosen curves.
ABOVE   The bare structure in winter.

Good buildings are often seen to improve as they mature – but this can never have been so literally the case as in the willow constructions of Marcel Kalberer, a Swiss-born architect who works in Germany. Kalberer's buildings literally grow into place, since they are living both at the time of construction and throughout their lives. Whereas the structure is evident from the beginning, the 'cladding' takes time to appear – and, indeed, disappears each winter. Kalberer exploits the extraordinary properties of willow, one of the easiest woods to grow. It can be harvested in winter as whips (long, slender branches) that are then put in the ground and will most probably take root and start to grow. Their flexibility means that the whips can be tied over frames or simply fastened together to form shapes.

Kalberer did not invent the idea of living construction. Popular in the UK and Scandinavia, and now being adopted in parts of the USA, it is often used to create living fences and children's play structures. At Grosvenor County primary school in Staffordshire, England, in another recreation of a traditional art, it has been used to make a maze, appropriately in the form of a Staffordshire knot. There are also designers who create living furniture, either using such materials as red alder to train a bush into a shape and then harvest it in finished form, or making garden furniture in willow that can then take root in a new location. What makes Kalberer special is that he brings an architect's sensibility and an interesting set of cultural references to his living buildings. He uses ideas drawn from Mesopotamian architecture to design his green buildings, creating interlinked systems of arches with pointed tops that seem part-Gothic and part-oriental.

Kalberer's first major construction was the Auerworld palace at Auerstedt near Weimar, built by 300 volunteers from all over the world in the spring of 1998. On this and subsequent projects, he has worked with a group of builders and constructors known as Sanfte Strukturen. The palace now serves as a focus for community events and has attracted more than 80,000 visitors to a very ordinary location, in particular to attend moon festivals. Kalberer has photographs of the festivals that show naked people frolicking among the greenery – an indication of the kind of Arcadian innocence mixed with mysticism for which he strives. Since this is the oldest of Kalberer's major willow constructions, the Auerworld palace is also the one that has filled in the most, with the growth of secondary and tertiary branches. Indeed, he has drawings of how he expects it to look up until 2012, when its shaggy, overgrown appearance almost entirely obscures the original structure. Like all

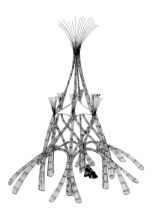

buildings, willow constructions require maintenance: twice a year, unrestrained branches must be tied in and any undesirable or dead growth trimmed.

Since Auerstedt, Kalberer has moved on to even more ambitious projects. Whereas the Auerworld palace has a circular plan, the Weidendom cathedral in Rostock has an almost conventional, cruciform church plan, with a nave and an apse. In fact, Kalberer's constructions are too ambitious to be constructed entirely of willow. Look closely at Auerworld and you will see some slender, steel circumferential elements, plus a crowning item, reminiscent of the spikes seen on the top of German dress helmets of the First World War. At the Weidendom, preformed steel tubing was used to support between 700 and 900 cubic metres (24,700 and 31,800 cubic feet) of willow, formed into arches up to 9 metres (30 feet) across. Huge numbers of volunteers also worked on this, and 600 of them completed the construction in two months, with no mechanical assistance. Ecumenical Christian and Jewish services were held in the building during the Rostock garden festival in 2003. To improve the level of shelter, tents were suspended within parts of the structure.

Kalberer employed a similar idea – of suspending a tent within a willow structure – at the Boo1 City of Tomorrow exhibition in Malmö, Sweden, which used a newly created city district on reclaimed industrial land to demonstrate sustainable approaches to building and city planning. Kalberer's pavilion, a single, tall Gothic element, formed the entrance to a series of 25 'secret gardens', set, appropriately, within a willow forest. But it also served as the shelter for Sweden's Crown Princess Victoria when she formally opened the exhibition – hence its name of Victoria Pavilion. Built only weeks before the start of the show, the pavilion was irrigated intensively, so that it started to grow almost at once.

Victoria Pavilion was a very temporary structure. Some of Kalberer's other shelters can expect a longer developmental period and lifespan, although none is likely to endure into the twenty-second century. But that is not the point. Providing some kind of shelter in summer, they are a means of getting in touch with nature and, one suspects, a whole raft of semi-mystical ideas. Once their time is past, through redundancy, collapse or death, they can (give or take a few bits of steel) simply rot down into the ground again.

TOP LEFT AND RIGHT

ABOVE

THIS PAGE
The Victoria Pavilion was built in 2001 as an entrance feature for the Boo1 City of Tomorrow exhibition in Malmö, Sweden, and to shelter Crown Princess Victoria at the opening.
The Weidendom cathedral was completed in 2001.

OPPOSITE
TOP LEFT   Like all Kalberer's work, the Weidendom draws on forms from Mesopotamian architecture.
TOP RIGHT   The plan of the cathedral, however, is close to that of a conventional Gothic church.
BOTTOM   Tents were suspended within the cathedral structure to provide extra shelter during the Rostock garden festival in 2003.

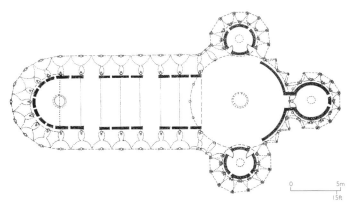

SHELTER

Campo de Vallemaggia, Ticino, Switzerland | Roberto Briccola | 2001

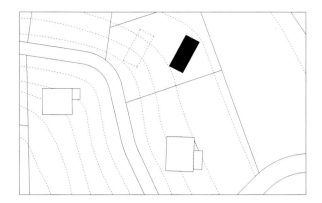

OPPOSITE

TOP   The deliberately asymmetric positioning of the openings in the four façades gives articulation to this simple building.

BOTTOM   (and this page above) Four concrete columns support the building, minimizing its interference with the ground beneath.

THIS PAGE

TOP LEFT   The shelter is sited at an angle to the contours, reducing the change in ground level and taking maximum advantage of the views.

TOP RIGHT   In contrast to the nearby log-built chalets, Briccola's design draws on the traditions of the grain barn.

BOTTOM RIGHT   External cladding consists of tongued-and-grooved larch planks.

Who wouldn't like a weekend house in the Ticino region of Switzerland? It offers pristine Alpine scenery, coupled with an Italian flavour to the language and the climate, which is warmer than elsewhere in Switzerland. The flora, a combination of Alpine and Mediterranean species, is one of the richest and most interesting in Europe. But building there carries heavy responsibilities. This is not a region devoid of architectural heritage – Mario Botta is one of its native sons – but in the most glorious places, precisely those places that might be desirable to spend a weekend, any kind of construction can feel like sacrilege.

Roberto Briccola has tackled the problem by designing a house that takes to an extreme the concept of 'touching the ground lightly' and is such an exquisitely crafted object that all but the most curmudgeonly of critics would see it as an enhancement of the landscape. Its smallness and austerity doubtless make the owners feel innocent of any charges of city sybaritism. Essentially a timber box measuring 48 square metres (520 square feet), the house sits level on four concrete columns of different heights to accommodate the slope of the site. The idea is that the meadowland beneath the house can continue to flourish, but its resilience when deprived of much of its sunlight and rain remains to be seen.

Although there are some traditional log-built chalet houses within sight, Briccola has drawn on a different tradition, that of the grain barn – which, because it is much more austere, has a greater appeal to contemporary sensibilities. Entrance is from the higher, northern side, with a metal-sheltered porch forming the only extrusion from the rectangular box shape. Internally, there are effectively two open spaces, stacked one above the other and joined by a spiral staircase in the northeast corner. The ground floor is a kitchen, dining and living area, with one small window along the west side, where the kitchen units are, and a larger one on the east to allow views out from the dining table. The whole of the southern end opens onto a balcony, sheltered by the floor above. In this way, the building takes advantage of

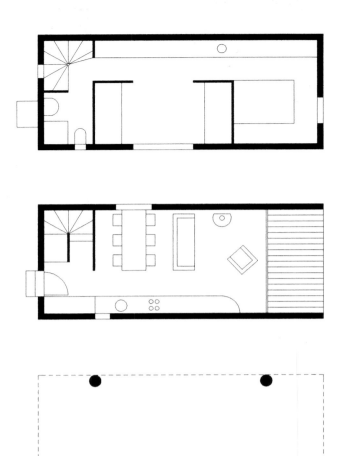

the best views, those to the south and east. The upper floor has a bathroom tucked into its northwest corner, a wardrobe running along the eastern wall and two sets of built-in bunks defining the spaces of two bedrooms. Windows are on the west and south sides, plus a north-facing window above the stair.

One of the pleasures of a building as small as this is that the architect solves the jigsaw puzzle of where to put the internal elements and these then remain fixed for all time. There is no room to permit flexibility and rearrangements, so the windows can be placed precisely to suit the use. This results in a pleasing, well-considered asymmetry on the perfectly rectangular façades.

The structural frame is of pine, with the exterior post-ventilated cladding in horizontal tongued-and-grooved larch planks. Internal cladding is of plywood for the roof, ceilings and floor. To ensure that the building's austerity does not tip over into discomfort, a reassuring mineral-wool insulation, 14 cm (5½ inches) thick, has been set into the walls, ceilings and floor. The weekend house at Campo de Vallemaggia is indeed a timber box, but one that, given the wonderful views that tempt people both to look out and to venture out, should never feel claustrophobic.

DOWNLAND GRIDSHELL

Sussex, England | Edward Cullinan Architects | 2002

The three-humped whale of the Downland Gridshell at the Weald and Downland Museum at Singleton in Sussex is a building that could only have happened at the start of the twenty-first century. A magnificent structure, a romantic gesture and a tour de force of engineering and innovation, it has a mass of contradictory attributes that add to. rather than detract from, the overall achievement.

The Weald and Downland Museum is an open-air collection of rescued rural buildings from the south of England, which have been reconstructed and refurnished. Native plants grow in the gardens, and rural crafts and traditions have been revived and re-enacted. Representing a past that has virtually disappeared, even if some of its physical fabric remains, the museum straddles, almost entirely successfully, the gap between education and entertainment, between a history lesson and a theme park. This is the setting for the gridshell. The most eye-catching construction on the site, it is the only significant new building, yet it has a workaday purpose. Many grandstanding buildings serve grandiose functions; by contrast, the gridshell is a combination of store and workshop.

Another sort of building could have satisfied the museum's needs at a far lower cost. A simple pole barn, a building clad in corrugated metal, would have been more typical of today's rural vernacular – and, in a sense, a more appropriate continuation of the pragmatic rural tradition that most of the museum's other buildings represent. But the museum had greater ambitions, and was able to satisfy them because, for a brief period, money was available in a way that it hadn't been for a long time previously, and probably won't be again, thanks to the launch in the 1990s of the UK National Lottery. Like all national lotteries, it attracted an initial surge of enthusiasm from the public that sent ticket sales soaring. This was coupled with a willingness by the British government, before complications set in, to put much of the money into the construction of new buildings. During the short-lived honeymoon period, the Weald and Downland Museum won a substantial grant from one of the distributing bodies, the Heritage Lottery Fund, that allowed it to envisage a far more adventurous building than it would otherwise have been able to do.

Since the workshop would be largely dedicated to reconstructing and refurbishing the timber frames of other buildings on the site, the building needed a large, clear span. This was achieved by a development of the technology pioneered by Frei Otto and engineer Buro Happold at the Mannheim garden festival in the 1970s.

OPPOSITE
Walls of the Downland Gridshell are clad with
locally grown red cedar planks.

THIS PAGE
RIGHT
Despite using advanced technology, the building sits
comfortably in its rustic setting.

BELOW
The form of the gridshell resembles two egg timers,
laid end to end.

Buro Happold, also the engineer on the gridshell project, had in the meantime acquired considerable experience of working with green (unseasoned) oak, the main material used in the museum structure. Increasingly sophisticated computer technology allowed calculations of a complexity that would not have been possible earlier. Yet at the same time the building process was remarkably 'hands on'. Members of the architect's team, developing the ideas from an unbuilt structure that was intended to form part of an exhibition at Paris's Pompidou Centre, were frequent visitors to the site. They were not merely inspecting progress. They were carrying out practical experiments to see whether the calculated forms were achievable in practice.

Edward Cullinan, the founder of the practice, has described the gridshell as

'far beyond Hi-Tech, in that it prophesies a new and ecological use of materials in the light of the knowledge gained during the last, high-technology century.' It is remarkably unwasteful of materials and has a hard logic underlying the romanticism of its form. The three-humped shape is in no sense whimsical. It provides a greater stability and hence economy of materials than a simple tunnel shape would have done.

Although the visitor is immediately aware of the timber structure, it is in fact only the upper layer of the building. The lower layer, the store, is a concrete structure, dug into the chalk hillside, and so energy-efficient that it needs only a simple domestic boiler to heat it. Glulam posts and beams support the heavy roof of the store, made of 80 mm (3 inch) tongued-and-grooved British spruce, which acts as the structural

diaphragm floor for the gridshell. The gridshell itself is the first double-layer timber gridshell in the UK and only the fifth worldwide. It is a doubly curved shell made from oak laths, 50 mm (2 inches) wide and 35 mm (3⅓ inches) thick, in four layers. Its double-hourglass shape, 48 metres (157 feet) long, is 16 metres (53 feet) across at its widest points and 11 metres (36 feet) wide at the waists. The internal height varies between 7 metres (23 feet) and 10 metres (33 feet).

Green oak was used because its high moisture content gives it great flexibility – essential during the forming process, since the laths in the gridshell were curved in both directions. Once the laths were in their final position, natural drying strengthened the structure. Oak, traditionally used for British boat building – and this structure in many

ways resembles an upturned boat – has the advantage of being twice as strong as equivalent sizes of other common timbers. This meant that smaller cross-sections could be used, and bent to the required radius, giving the whole structure a lighter look, and more than offsetting the fact that the oak required a higher bending force to achieve the desired curvature.

Ironically, given the underlying ethos that materials should as far as possible be sourced locally, the oak had to be imported. The UK had achieved its deforestation centuries before anybody started to worry about the depletion of the Amazon jungle, and there were no adequate supplies in the densely populated southeast of the country. British timber would have had to travel long distances by road. It was decided that it would be 'greener' to import the

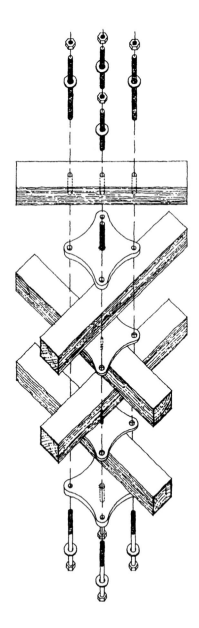

wood from Normandy, in France, just across the English Channel, where there are sustainable plantations.

It was essential that there were no defects in the oak laths. Natural defects in the wood were therefore cut out, and the remaining short lengths of timber were reconnected into 6 metre (20 foot) lengths using finger joints, which could be produced quickly and cheaply with minimum waste. The success of these finger joints relied in part on the latest in glue technology, which could accommodate the high moisture content of up to 40 per cent in the green oak. In contrast, the 6 metre (20 foot) lengths were then joined on site using traditional scarf joints to produce continuous laths – up to 37 metres (121 feet) long for the lattice laths and 50 metres (164 feet) long for the longitudinal rib laths. These scarf joints were similar to the techniques used on many of the historic buildings that make up the museum collection.

The gridshell was built flat on top of a special lightweight scaffold that stood on the timber floor and was then carefully pulled down into position and fixed. The architect and engineer worked closely with the contractor, the Green Oak Carpentry Company, which devised one of the most essential elements – a pinless connecting device for the laths, which gives them stability, but allows the

necessary degree of movement. The device consists of three plates. The centre plate has pins simply to locate the grid geometry of the middle lath layers, and the outer plates loosely hold the outer laths in place, allowing sliding during the formation of the shell. Two of the four bolts locating the plates were used to connect the diagonal bracing, bolted in place to provide shear stiffness after the shell had been formed. Green Oak has now patented this device.

In areas of high load, the laths were spaced 50 cm (20 inches) apart. Over the rest of the structure, this was increased to 1 metre (3 feet). Once the gridshell had been formed – the most exciting and nerve-racking part of the process – additional, diagonal bracing was added, consisting of longitudinal and transverse timber rib-laths, fixed to the nodes to provide shear resistance and to 'lock in' the shape. The bracing also supports the wall and roof cladding. Shear blocks were screwed into place between the layers of the shell. In this way, parallel lines of laths act compositely; the sizes and positions of the shear blocks were arranged to suit the forces determined by computer analysis. Only at this stage could the last of the temporary props be removed.

The success of the finger-jointing technique was demonstrated by the fact that, with some 10,000 finger-joints

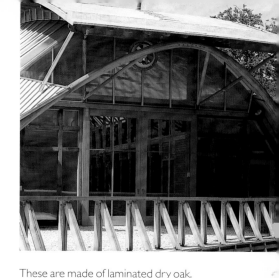

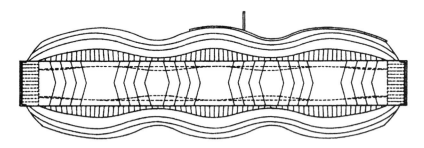

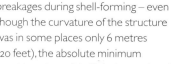

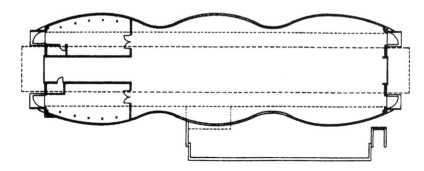

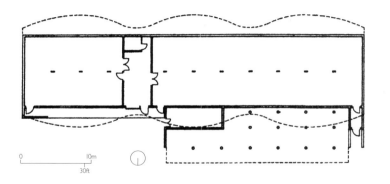

0   10m
30ft

in the structure, there were only 145 breakages during shell-forming – even though the curvature of the structure was in some places only 6 metres (20 feet), the absolute minimum considered possible. Repairs consisted of introducing solid blocking between laths at the point of failure.

The cladding is locally grown red cedar planks; there is an aluminium foil inner lining, with insulation between the two. The roof is a 'ribbon roof' consisting of 100 mm (4 inch) x 12 mm (¼ inch) longitudinal timbers, laid at 200 mm (9 inch) centres across a support frame. Fir was used for this frame because it combines durability with availability in small sections of the long lengths required. On top of the timber is a waterproof, reinforced-polythene barrier, backed with foil, then a multi-layer insulation material laid into a void, a 12 mm (¼ inch) plyboard and a further layer of 12 mm (¼ inch) ply, covered with a cementitious reinforced material called Roofcrete. Between the cladding and the roof is a deep layer of clerestory glazing, made of polycarbonate, since the degree of movement in the structure precluded the use of glass. Catenary arches at each end of the building form the support for awnings.

These are made of laminated dry oak.

A well-thought-out environmental strategy minimizes the use of energy for heating and cooling the building. For the museum, the gridshell is much more than just a building fit for its purpose. It is also a reflection of the institution's aims, an icon and a draw in its own right. The museum has made the most of this, using the gridshell to hold weekend seminars on timber. On its website, at http://www.wealddown.co.uk/downland-gridshell-construction-progress.htm, there is a detailed description, in words and pictures, of the construction process.

In 2002, the gridshell was a runner-up for the Stirling Prize, the UK's most prestigious award for architecture. It was narrowly beaten by an urban steel footbridge. The function and appearance of the two projects could not be more different, but each exemplifies the spirit of innovation in UK architecture at the start of the twenty-first century. That this innovative spirit can find expression in a material as redolent of history and tradition as timber is a tribute to the imagination and dedication of the team involved in the design and construction of the gridshell.

PAINTROCK CAMP
Hyattville, Wyoming, USA | Charles Rose Architects | 2000

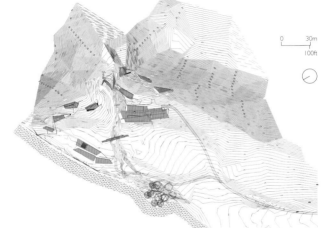

The vast size and magnificent scenery of the USA mean that, if a charitable foundation wishes to give inner-city children a taste of country life, it can take them somewhere truly remote. Paintrock Camp at Hyattville, Wyoming, is such a project. Sponsored by the Alm Foundation, the private foundation of the chief executive of Coca-Cola Enterprises, it allows 76 young people from Los Angeles schools to enjoy horse riding, trekking and other outdoor activities during their summer vacation.

Set at the base of two converging canyons in the Big Horn mountains, Paintrock Camp is part of a 44,000 hectare (110,000 acre) ranch. With its substantial accommodation, plus facilities that include stables, a dining hall, a swimming pool and recreational areas, it could have required a very large building. But this would have been against the spirit of the place. Instead, Charles Rose Architects have created a number of separate structures. Oriented in a way that looks almost random, they are, in fact, carefully placed to take the best advantage of views and to respond to the contours of the land, so that, although the residents have a sense of enclosure and of access to other parts of the site on elevated walkways, they are constantly in touch with the outdoor world that they have come to Paintrock Camp to experience. By raising most of the buildings on stilts, the architect has reduced the impact

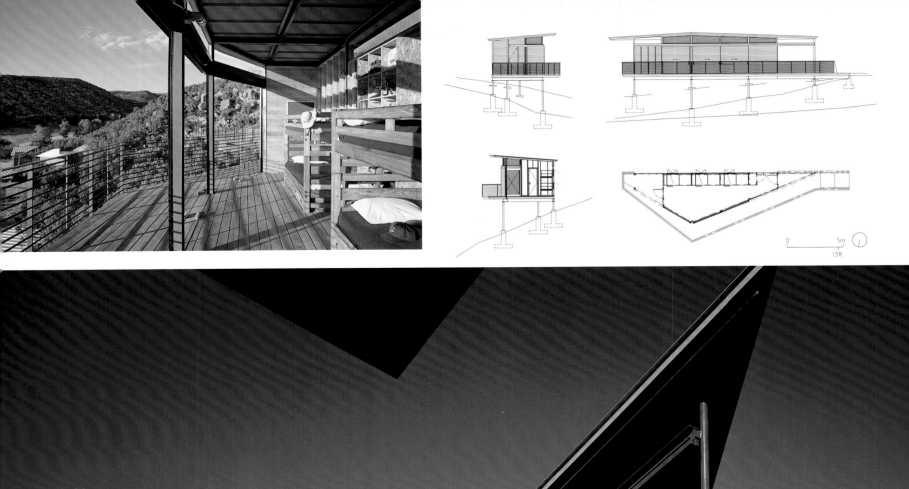

OPPOSITE

TOP LEFT   One side of the sleeping cabins can open up entirely in good weather.

TOP RIGHT   Sections and plans of a typical sleeping cabin.

BOTTOM   Steel-framed and standing on steel platforms, the sleeping cabins are clad with western red cedar.

THIS PAGE

ABOVE   The windows have wooden shutters.

RIGHT   Student accommodation and the dining hall make up the main eastern camp. Housing for the camp staff and visitors is placed to the west. To the southwest are the stables and an offloading shelter for arrivals and departures.

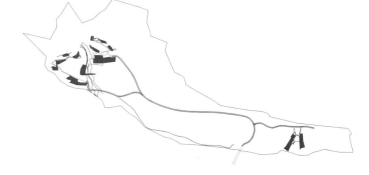

0   120m
400ft

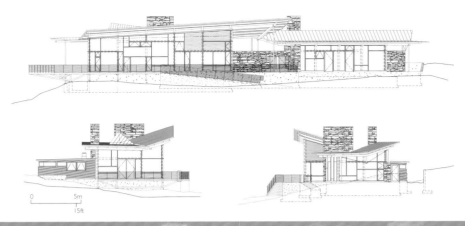

OPPOSITE

TOP LEFT   Recycled Douglas fir beams support the butterfly
             roof of the dining hall.

TOP RIGHT   Long section and cross sections through the dining
             hall, the largest building in the camp and its social
             centre.

BOTTOM   Timber frames the glazing of the dining-hall walls.

THIS PAGE

ABOVE   External sloping columns support the roof of the
             stable block.

TOP RIGHT   Inside the stable block, walls and stalls are clad in
             timber.

on the ground, and its use of platforms and walkways creates a series of spaces for informal interaction, or simply for standing and gazing, which make up a crucial part of the experience.

Most of the accommodation is contained in the main, eastern camp. Some way away, to the west, is housing for the camp director and for guests. And to the southwest, near the boundary of the site, are the stables and an offloading shelter to deal with arrivals and departures.

In the eastern camp, there are two clusters of student accommodation, connected by a bridge. Each cluster comprises three sleeping cabins for boys and three for girls, with a shower block for each cluster. Supported on steel platforms, the steel-framed cabins are roughly triangular in shape. They are compact, with bunk beds and storage all built in timber, and stand on a timber deck. The material used throughout is western red cedar. The cladding is of horizontal planks, and there are large rolling doors that can be opened completely in fine weather. On the opposite side are small timber shutters that open out from the wall – with the guarantee of a dramatic view outside.

The dining hall forms the largest building in this grouping. Standing on a concrete foundation, and with some stone walls and a stone fireplace and chimney, it is nevertheless a largely timber-framed structure, with butterfly metal roofs supported on recycled Douglas fir beams and an almost Mondrian-like pattern of framing to the glazed walls. Recycled Douglas fir has also been used on the stables complex, where, externally, hockey-stick columns support the sloping roofs. There is a sheltered entrance between the two sets of stables, which are set at right angles to each other, and a combination of timber and corrugated metal cladding externally. Inside, the walls and stalls are clad in timber. The restricted palette of materials gives an architectural unity to the camp, in a manner that is far more pleasing and appropriate to the surroundings than any rigidly planned grid would have been. The camp engages continually with its environment, while creating a series of spaces and shelters that is both reassuring and intriguing.

REEVE RESIDENCE

Lopez Island, Washington, USA | Cutler Anderson Architects | 2002

OPPOSITE

TOP   Architect James Cutler sited and designed the
              building to minimize its visual impact on the
              surrounding landscape.

BOTTOM   A green roof, sloping at the angle of least resistance
              to the prevailing wind, minimizes drag and visibility
              from further up the slope.

THIS PAGE

ABOVE   Sketch showing how easily the house fits into the
              landscape.

TOP RIGHT   A retaining wall of moss stone from Montana assists
              with the camouflage.

There are generally two groups of people who want houses on islands. One group dreams of a tropical climate, a beach and palm trees. The other wants to be in touch with raw nature, to be buffeted by the wind and stimulated by ever-changing views. Lopez is the kind of island that appeals to the second group. The largest, flattest and most sparsely populated of the three San Juan Islands in Washington state, off the west coast of the USA, it may have an organic food store and good internet access, but it is still a rugged spot, an ideal place for watching orca whales and bald eagles. With regular ferry services, Lopez is a popular holiday and weekend destination for people from Seattle, who enjoy its sunnier climate, as well as its other advantages.

When Sally and Tom Reeve, two Seattle residents, decided to build a house on Lopez, they chose to do so on the southern tip, the most rugged part of the island. With architect Jim Cutler, they set about selecting a suitable spot. He dissuaded them from their original choice, on top of a ridge. As well as being exposed to the winds, which often reach 110 km (70 miles) per hour, such a position would, says Cutler, 'have desecrated the cliff'. Instead, he moved them to a less obvious place, between rocky outcrops, with a forest to the north and the Pacific Ocean to the south. The principal view from the coast

is of the house's retaining wall in a moss stone brought in from Montana. Surprisingly, the moss stone blends better with the surrounding lichen-covered rocks than does the local stone, which is far too white. The other most visible element is the roof, which covers the entire property. Treetops here are often sheared off by the wind, so the architect gave the roof a low pitch, set at a similar angle to that of the sheared treetops. As well as making the roof less visually intrusive, this also reduces its wind resistance. Supported on a timber deck, and highly insulated, the roof is mostly covered in turf sod, planted with local plants for increased camouflage.

Beneath the roof are three pavilions, all angled slightly differently to take advantage of the views. But all face roughly south, to the sea. The central, largest pavilion contains the kitchen and a massive living room. To the east is the 'master suite' for the family, and to the west is the bunkhouse, designed compactly to house up to 12 visitors – and visitors must be common in this delightful location. The separate pavilions means that, when seen from the north, the house does not present a single impenetrable wall, but allows views through passages to the ocean.

The variation in the pavilions has been made possible by placing the major elements of the structure outside them,

so that the walls have to support only their own weight. Beams and columns are made of four pieces of fir, flitched with steel, chiefly at the connection points. On the northern side, where the roof is highest, the columns are cross-braced. In recognition of the composite nature of the construction, each X-shaped brace consists of one wooden element and one galvanized-steel plate, joined at the centre with a shear connector and a through bolt.

The building is clad with cedar shingles, although on the southern façade there is as much glazing as possible. This reaches its apogee in the main, central pavilion, where the timber-framed windows slide back to create an opening nearly 5 metres (16 feet) in width. Internally, timber is widely used, with white-pine wall cladding and built-in furniture contrasting with the darker wood of the underside of the roof. In an expression of hedonism, the building has a hot pool on the seaward side, and the stone terrace that links the pavilions is heated, so that those walking from one to another with bare feet will not suffer.

The house won an award from the Seattle chapter of the American Institute of Architects and a Wood Design Award. In their citation, the judges said, 'The home is a truly sustainable building because it starts with nature. It merges with the rock and flora of the landscape as if it grew there.'

Y HOUSE

Catskill Mountains, New York, USA | Steven Holl Architects | 1999

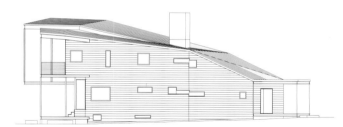

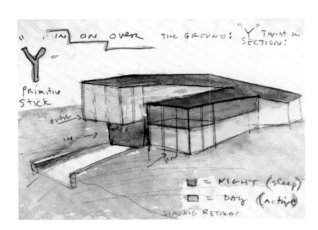

TOP   The twisted geometry of the Y House elevations allows it to take maximum advantage of views and redefines the conventional idea of how a house is used.

BOTTOM   Clad in red-painted cedar, and with its steel frame the colour of red oxide, the building makes reference to nearby stables.

THIS PAGE

ABOVE   In one of his characteristic watercolour sketches, Holl based his design on a Y-shaped stick, and defined zones for use during the day and at night.

RIGHT   The living-room balcony, on the west wing, oversails the partly buried children's bedrooms.

For an architect like Steven Holl, whose primary architectural interest is in designing to take advantage of changing light, the site for the Y House must have been nearly ideal. Located in the Catskill mountains, in New York State, it stands on a rising piece of ground and offers views of two different valleys. Holl designed a house that exploited the views and challenged ideas of how a house 'ought' to be, while accommodating the specific requirements of his clients.

In addition to the usual desire of weekenders for a great location within fairly easy reach of the city (New York City is a couple of hours' drive away), the owners wanted somewhere to store and display part of their art collection. Holl gave them a house of just over 325 square metres (3,500 square feet), with a double-height foyer space, ideal for showing art, which splits into two wings, distinguished from each other by their degree of privacy. In common with most of Holl's other projects, the design arose from a series of watercolour sketches. Holl likes to develop these over a period, sometimes several months. 'These sketches are indispensable for me to consider at the same time the conceptual idea, the texture, the colours and the light,' he says. 'At first, I am above all interested in defining where the light comes from and how it moves. In this way, I can already, from the first sketch, prefigure a certain

THIS PAGE

BELOW LEFT The angle between the two wings allows each to have views along a different valley.

BELOW RIGHT From bottom, ground-floor, first-floor and roof plans show the games that Holl has played with geometry and the customary disposition of spaces.
1. living room, 2. master bedroom, 3. bedroom, 4. dining room

OPPOSITE
The roofs run down towards the entrance, where rainwater is collected in a cistern.

complexity of possible conditions. Sometimes I will work on numerous sketches and theories before convincing myself definitely to take a certain path.'

For this house in the Catskills, he developed an idea from what he called a 'primitive stick', resembling a catapult. He then defined zones of day and night, and twisted the axis of his 'Y', so that its stem was almost at right angles to its centre line. He was also very interested in the building's relationship with the ground: some parts are within the ground, others stand on it, and others fly over it. The east wing has the dining room at ground level, with the master bedroom above it. In the west wing, the children's bedrooms are set into the ground, with the living room above

them and oversailing them. By putting the two wings at an acute angle to each other, Holl allowed each to face directly towards one of the valleys, and also created a kind of chasm between them that brings in ever-changing light.

The building is steel-framed and steel-roofed, with the steel painted the colour of red oxide. It is clad in cedar, also painted red – a reference in material and colour to the stables of the surrounding farms. At the end of each wing, facing almost due south, are deep balconies, with roofs above them. These balconies are one above the other on the east wing, but on the west wing there is a balcony only on the upper level, projecting beyond the children's rooms below. As well as providing a

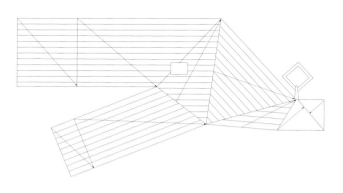

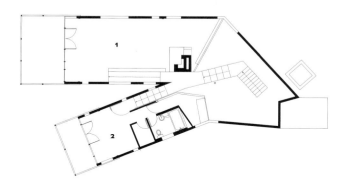

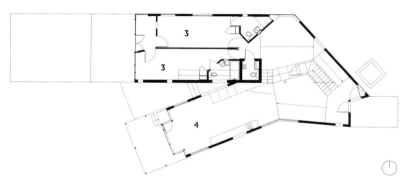

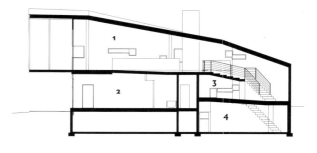

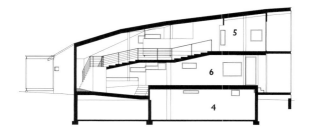

OPPOSITE
Ash is used for the floors and stair treads in the foyer.

THIS PAGE

ABOVE   Long sections through the west wing (top) and east wing (centre); cross sections through the foyers (above left) and the wings (above right).

RIGHT   Changes in level and orientation are most obvious at the point where the foyer bifurcates.

KEY   1. living room, 2. bedroom, 3. foyers, 4. basement, 5. master bedroom, 6. dining room

satisfactory termination to the forward and upward thrust of the house, the large overhangs allow in the winter sun, while providing shade in high summer. As the roofs run downward all the way to the entrance, rain is channelled back to there and collected in a cistern.

Internally, the house has ash floors and stair treads. Ceilings in the foyer are also of wood. The double-height entrance foyer is spatially complex, and it is there that the irregular disposition of windows, designed to make the most of the views, is most evident. Appropriately, perhaps, for a space intended for the display of art, there is a somewhat institutional feel, accentuated by the variation in levels.

Steven Holl has created a house that takes maximum advantage of its magnificent position, and which must interact with its ever-changing surroundings. It is an extravagant house, with a large external surface relative to its volume, costly in terms both of materials and energy consumption. Neither are its games with the levels of sleeping accommodation as revolutionary as one might first imagine. A cynic would simply see the children tucked away on the ground floor, and the service spaces pushed even lower into the basement, while the adults enjoyed all the best spaces. But as a luxury weekend retreat that responds to its site, it must be a great pleasure for Holl's clients to inhabit.

OPPOSITE
Carl-Viggo
Hølmebakk's summer
house at Risør,
Norway, reinterprets
the vernacular with
references to
Norway's classical
tradition and the use
of contemporary
construction
techniques.

Across great swathes of the world, timber was, for many centuries, the natural building material, the people's medium of choice. If wood was readily available, as it was in many temperate and tropical zones until deforestation, then it was used for all but the humblest of everyday buildings. The tools to work it were not sophisticated and would probably have been available to anybody accustomed to harvesting timber as fuel. Timber buildings were both durable and affordable.

As a result, a profusion of forms of vernacular timber construction have arisen. These have been affected by such diverse considerations as climate, the types of timber available and the randomness of historical development. In some places, the tradition of building with wood has virtually disappeared – London, for example, lost its timber buildings in the Great Fire of 1666 and issued ordinances to prevent their replacement. On the other hand, Helsinki, Finland's modern, forward-looking capital, carefully preserves an area of traditional log houses, sandwiched between busy urban highways. And in rural areas of many countries, the traditional forms remain, from the chalets of Switzerland to the coconut-wood shelters of Samoa. One of the pleasures of travel is to see how different cultures have used the same material in different ways.

How can those traditions be reinterpreted today? There are too many twee and unimaginative responses. In the USA, groups of enthusiasts are reviving cordwood masonry, building houses from what look like bundles of firewood. While their technical rediscoveries are fascinating, the architecture is, frankly, hideous and incongruous. In many other places, pastiche has created lifeless architecture, ill-suited to the twenty-first century.

But there is another way of approaching the vernacular. Architects can take elements of traditional architecture and incorporate them into buildings that are very much of the moment. In the countryside around Granada, Spain, Eduardo y Luis Javier Martín Martín have created a house that follows the form of traditional agricultural buildings and uses traditional materials, but is as far as it is possible to get from an unsympathetic barn conversion (see page 66). The architects have offered a compact and supremely rational way of living, within a restricted envelope.

In creating a Norwegian summer house, traditionally known as a 'hutte', Carl-Viggo Hølmebakk has used a 1,000-year-old technique of employing timber wedges to level the foundations, and has clad the building

in Norwegian larch. But, by the adoption of prefabrication and the extremely precise detailing, he has given the building a modern twist, while the coherence of his plan draws strongly on the Norwegian classical tradition.

In Switzerland, Foster and Partners have used the traditional Swiss building material to create an apartment block that seems futuristic and is designed using the most advanced computer technology (see page 70). Yet it takes advantage of window details traditional to the Engadin valley and is clad in larch shingles, cut by traditionally trained craftsmen, as part of a strategy to make the building as environmentally sustainable as possible.

Swiss architect Peter Zumthor also used traditional techniques in his Hanover Expo pavilion (see page 56), although these were drawn more from cabinetmaking than from common building practice. And, rather than seeking durability, he designed a structure in which all the elements could be taken away and reused – presumably in more traditional building types.

At Chessy in France, Avant Travaux was concerned less with traditional techniques than with well-established building forms. It recreated the pitched

roofs and freestanding nature of the *pavillons* beloved of the French bourgeoisie (see page 52). This may have been a slightly childlike interpretation, but why not? The architect was, after all, designing a centre for children.

Most intriguing, perhaps, is the Sami parliament building in the north of Norway (see page 60). The Sami have no architectural tradition, having lived a nomadic existence, so in commissioning a parliament building they were also looking to create a national architecture. Drawing on the forms of tents and reindeer stockades, the architects, Stein Halvorsen and Christian A. Sundby, have reinterpreted these familiar structures on a larger and more permanent scale. For the Sami, timber is not a traditional material to be superseded by more permanent and weighty materials, such as stone and brick. Instead, it represents a step towards a more settled existence than they knew before and an attempt to create an identifiable architectural language alongside a system of government and representation. As well as drawing on traditions, the architects have created what may be the vernacular of tomorrow.

CHILDREN'S LEISURE CENTRE
Chessy, France | Avant Travaux | 2002

OPPOSITE

TOP   Well-established trees brush against the roofs of
           the new buildings.
BOTTOM   Two of the buildings intersect.

THIS PAGE

RIGHT   Pastel colours soften the fairly simplistic forms.
BELOW   Pitched roofs create play areas and observation
           spaces, either enclosed or open.

Chessy, in the Ile de France, is only a stone's throw from Disneyland Paris at Marne la Vallée, but prides itself on being a world apart. Endowed with some historic buildings and plenty of trees and greenery, it promotes itself as a country town, despite the fact that it is rapidly being swallowed up by the Parisian agglomeration.

Mickey Mouse has no place here, but the children's leisure centre has been built in gardens that formerly belonged to the creator of a character equally famous among French children. Jean de Brunhoff was the creator of Babar the elephant. There is something of the enchanted dream of childhood about the leisure centre, but with none of Disney's brashness. At Chessy, children enjoy buildings that are like every child's drawing of a house, only more so. The three linked buildings, with tall, pitched roofs, have been positioned carefully among the existing trees, so that none needed to be cut down. The result is that birches, several gingko biloba and a magnificent cherry push right up against the roofs of the buildings, allowing the sensation from inside of being in a structure more akin to a tree house than a Wendy house. Two of the buildings are side by side, with one effectively cutting into the other. The third is positioned further back, and a discreet entrance is placed between the three, designed so that it maintains the sense of separate structures.

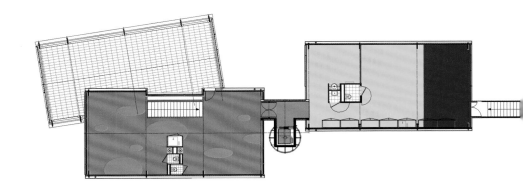

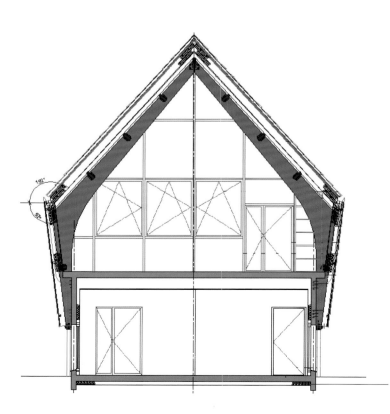

The buildings' roofs are not only taller than those on conventional houses, but also inhabitable, making them effectively upper storeys. Glulam beams were used to create the high pitch of the roofs, which are reminiscent of upturned boats. There are magnificent views out of the gable ends – glazed in the most enclosed of the structures and open in the others, with a railing against which to lean and gaze. While one of the three buildings has a conventional closed-in roof, the other two have strips of metal that provide some shade and changing light patterns for what is effectively an outdoor play area. Dreamy, pearlized colours are used on the roof coverings, and there are bright elements internally. For the 80 children who use the centre, the experience should be life-enhancing and mind-stretching. Chessy is the kind of place inhabited by those French people who have embraced the dream of a *pavillon*, a stand-alone residence in a plot of land, away from the cheek-by-jowl existence of the city centre or the more contemporary soullessness of the HLMs (large housing schemes on the edges of cities). In their play and their interaction with nature, their children may be acquiring similar tastes. The *pavillon* is not the most sustainable form of urban planning, but this children's equivalent is enchanting. To create such charm without tipping over into sentimentality is the considerable achievement of these buildings, which evoke childhood stories without becoming over-explicit.

SWISS PAVILION

Hanover Expo, Germany | Peter Zumthor | 2000

If the term 'magic realism' could be applied to architecture as easily as it is to literature, then Swiss architect Peter Zumthor would be seen as its chief exponent. He uses materials austerely and with tremendous care to create buildings of apparent simplicity that have a special extra element, a spirit and a feeling to them. His concerns are not limited to materiality and light, but embrace sound and smell as well, to create an all-round experience that embeds itself in the visitor's memory. Perhaps his most famous work is the thermal baths at Vals, but he also has several wood buildings to his name and has worked with wood since his youth.

The son of a furniture-maker, Zumthor himself trained as a cabinetmaker, and brought this experience to bear most directly in his design of the Swiss pavilion at the Hanover Expo of 2000. Mindful of the white elephants that had remained in other cities decades after the end of their Expos, the Germans decided that — with the odd exception, such as Thomas Herzog's canopy (see pages 136) — all the buildings should be temporary.

As a country that has seriously embraced the idea of waste elimination and recycling, Germany decreed that the national pavilions should be not only demountable, but also reusable. One of the most literal interpretations of this concept, Zumthor's Swiss pavilion was

effectively a stack of construction timber that would season during the period of the Expo and could then be taken down and used wherever else it was needed. The building was anything but prosaic. Designed like a maze, the square pavilion was intended to entertain, rather than confuse. Blocks of parallel walls, some oriented north–south and some east–west, enclosed a series of openings, some of which were simple courtyards and others three-storey oval metal structures, allowing visitors to go up spiral stairs to platforms. The walls were made of freshly cut timber baulks, longitudinally of pine and crossways of smaller elements of larch. The lattices

that these created allowed air to circulate freely – an ideal environment for seasoning the timber. No nails, screws or glue were used to hold the elements of the lattice together, since these would have diminished the potential for reuse. Instead, Zumthor used stainless-steel rods in tension to give stability to the stacks. With every element sharply defined, the crisp springs at the top provided an industrial aesthetic reminiscent of electricity isolators.

Zumthor anticipated that, during the course of the Expo, the timber stacks would decrease in height by 120 cm (47 inches) from drying out and compression. As a result, the tension in the steel rods fell with time. The only other elements in the building were lengths of galvanized gutters forming the roof. With the aroma of the drying timber and the drumming on the guttering during storms, smell and sound had already been added to the visual aspects of the design. Zumthor augmented these sensations as part of his unusual approach to the function of the building. By the time that the Hanover Expo was being planned, after some rather prosaic shows, such as that in Lisbon, the organizers had grasped that these exhibitions had to be more than just glorified trade fairs or a chance for countries to show off their wares. But, despite the greater sophistication and simplicity of the Hanover Expo, it

was still a fairly exhausting experience for visitors. Zumthor's idea was that the Swiss pavilion should offer them some respite, a chance to recharge their batteries. Calling his pavilion a Sound Box, he described it as 'an event of the sensuous kind. Architecture, sounds, words, food, drink and dress blend together in a mix of theatre and excitement to create a complete happening.' Musicians played in some of the courtyards, actors staged events and cooks created dishes, all under the direction of the architect. 'We will offer a representation in real time for the relaxation of tired visitors,' Zumthor wrote before the Expo opened. 'When they have attentively visited the first 50 pavilions, they will be able to recharge themselves with us. Like this, after half an hour they will be ready for the next 50 pavilions.'

There was nothing obviously Swiss in Zumthor's pavilion, except for the timber itself, which came from Swiss trees. But, for many busy people, Switzerland has been a place of regeneration and recuperation, whether in the tuberculosis sanatoria of the past or in the ski slopes and walking trails of today. And the country's own successful Expo in 2002 showed that this is a country that can combine meticulous organization with a capacity to surprise and delight – again, very much in the spirit of Zumthor's pavilion.

THIS PAGE
LEFT   Zumthor calculated that, during the length of the Expo, drying out would cause the walls to decrease in height by 120 cm (47 inches).
BELOW   The quality of light filtering in was a vital part of the experience.

OPPOSITE
Three-storey oval metal structures in some of the courtyards of the pavilion offered a different experience.

PARLIAMENT BUILDING

Karasjok, Norway | Stein Halvorsen and Christian A. Sundby | 2000

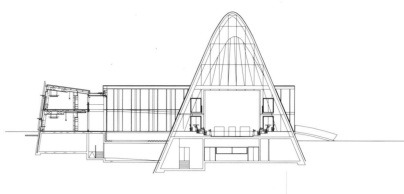

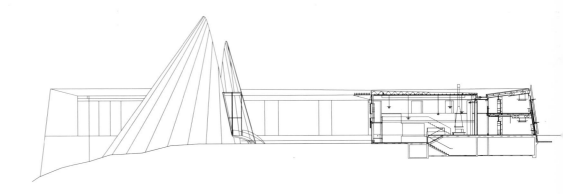

The Sami people of northern Norway and Finland (Lapland) are traditionally nomadic, so when they settle and want to erect buildings of civic significance, they have little tradition on which to draw. It is not surprising, therefore, that two representations of their nomadic life have informed the most significant building yet: the Sameting, or parliament building, in Karasjok, Norway, near the Finnish border. The traditional tepee-like tent, known as the *lavvo*, and the stockade used to enclose reindeer might seem too modest and workaday to fulfil a larger function. But the architects of the Sameting, who are based in Oslo, have adapted these forms into a building of great dignity and gravitas, which forms a vital focus in a town where most of the other development has been random and without architectural merit.

The dominant element is the debating chamber, which is based on a Sami tent. Its conical structure, clad in rough, untreated larch, looks rather like a rough-hewn, but carefully considered, woodstack. The cone is divided vertically into two unequal segments by a glass bridge. On the larger side is the debating chamber itself; on the smaller, an anteroom and access to the viewing gallery. The two vertical walls created by this slit are glazed, allowing light into the spaces, while maintaining the relatively closed exterior presence.

The rest of the building – based on a reindeer stockade – is in the form of a semicircle, with larger spaces for the Sami national library and a cafeteria contained within its embrace. The outer side of the semicircle has a battered, inward-sloping wall. Rough larch, the same as that on the debating chamber, is used to clad this part of the building, but here it runs horizontally instead of vertically. Since the building has only a simple timber canopy over the relatively modest entrance, reminiscent of the tent flap of the *lavvo* – or, in a more urban comparison, an up-and-over garage door – there is no strong sense of invitation. This is an inward-looking building in the style of traditional Sami dwellings. In one of the coldest places on earth, where there are months of darkness and winter temperatures fall regularly to below -50°c (-58°F), and which is infested by mosquitoes in summer, even the simplest structure acts as a refuge from the outside, rather than expressing a need to relate to it.

Internally, the story is very different. Offices and committee rooms occupy the outer, relatively blind face. In the centre of the building, facing onto a courtyard, is a two-level gallery used for informal meetings, strolling and unplanned interaction. It has some brightly coloured furniture, and the sense of colour is enhanced on important occasions when the Sami

wear national dress in red, yellow and green. Referring to the nomadic history of the Sami people, and described as a 'wander hall', it plays an important role in providing a sense of community. After all, for much of the year, there is unlikely to be much social interaction on the cold, dark streets of the town.

The largest spaces are the library and the café. Their roof is supported by glulam beams, up to 80 cm (32 inches) deep, with a span of up to 14 metres (46 feet). Steel columns support these beams, although where they meet the exterior glazing they are insulated and clad in wood to prevent the formation of cold bridges. Glulam is also used extensively in the debating chamber

building, with glulam arches and beams springing from a concrete ring beam.

Unfinished pine – though in a much more elegant and finished form than the external cladding – is used to clad the debating chamber interior. Thick fibreglass insulation keeps out the cold, as does the relatively low proportion of glazing. Cold air falling down from the surface of the glass is forced up again by heated air emerging from beneath the seats. Pine is also evident externally. In pressure-treated form, it is used as firings to support the rough larch. It provides enough ventilation behind the façade to allow the larch to dry out after rain. Since the larch is untreated, it will weather in time to a silver-grey colour.

THIS PAGE

ABOVE LEFT   The debating chamber is clad in rough, untreated larch.

ABOVE   View through the debating chamber glazing to the other side of the split cone.

OPPOSITE
The corridor on the inner side of the curved block is also a space for social interaction.

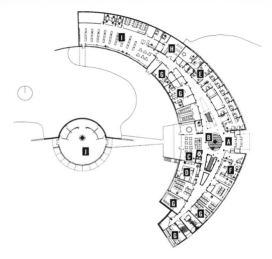

OPPOSITE

TOP LEFT The interior of the library, which has deep glulam beams.

TOP RIGHT Plan of the shared campus building of the Nicola Valley Institute of Technology and the University College of the Cariboo in British Columbia, Canada, showing an uncanny similarity to the plan of the Sami Parliament.

BOTTOM Unfinished pine cladding gives a warm feeling to the impressive debating chamber, with focus towards the glazed wall.

THIS PAGE

BELOW From bottom, ground- and first-floor plans of the parliament building show its stockade-like nature.

RIGHT Bright furniture adds a touch of colour to the predominantly timber-coloured spaces.

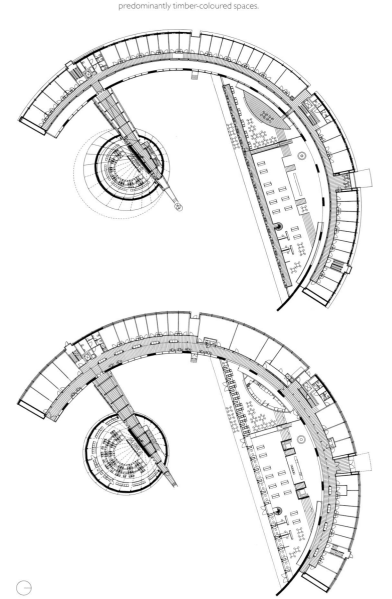

This magnificent building seems to be a solution to an issue unique in a modern western country: how to create an architectural identity for a people with little architectural history of their own. The Sami see their situation as similar to that of Native Americans, for example. In fact, the form of this building is not quite as unusual as it first appears. At a shared campus for the Nicola Valley Institute of Technology and the University College of the Cariboo in British Columbia, Canada, native and non-native students occupy the same space. The design, by architects Busby + Associates, was produced in consultation with local aboriginal elders. The resulting building also makes great use of wood. More surprising is the fact that, in plan, it is remarkably similar to the Sami parliament. It puts the main accommodation into a semicircular building, connected to a planned smaller circular space, which will be used as a ceremonial arbour. At Karasjok, of course, the parliamentary chamber – most certainly a ceremonial area – occupies the circular space. Could it be that a new architectural form is emerging in response to a set of sensitivities and requirements that previously were scarcely considered? If so, these two buildings, so far apart in Europe and America, will be seen as worthy pioneers.

COUNTRY HOUSE

Granada, Spain | Eduardo y Luis Javier Martín Martín | 2001

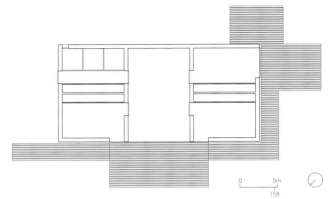

0   5m
15ft

OPPOSITE

TOP   The architects maximized the use of a restricted area by doing away with circulation space altogether.

BOTTOM   On the northern façade, glazing runs the full width of the central living room, and also extends to the bedrooms. Black poplar cladding recalls the vernacular of tobacco barns.

THIS PAGE

ABOVE   By making almost every opening a door, the architects maximized accessibility.

RIGHT   Decking, in a carefully considered configuration, effectively increases the footprint of the building.

The Moorish city of Granada in Andalucía, southern Spain, has a spectacular setting on the edge of the Sierra Nevada. Many visitors find that the backdrop of mountains enhances their experience of the Alhambra, but they may give less consideration to the fertile plains and meadows that stretch to the west of the city. In fact, this area, the Granada Vega, which occupies the basin of the Genil river, is also of historic importance, having long supported the city through its agriculture. And because of the special setting of Granada, the Vega is protected in a way that few such flat agricultural areas are.

Building a house there is not a straightforward business, and when the architects Eduardo y Luis Javier Martín Martín wanted to create a home for a client on the ruins of an agricultural building, they were limited to the volume of the building that they replaced. This gave them only 75 square metres (810 square feet) of space, on a single storey, which proved a wonderful discipline. Charged with producing a house with no wasted space, and no clutter, that would fit in with the agricultural vernacular, they produced an elegant, symmetrical building that sits comfortably in its surroundings, deals intelligently with the climate, and offers such a simple model for living that it makes many larger houses seem pokey and unnecessarily complex.

The first move was to eliminate all circulation space. Built to a very straightforward plan, the house is divided into three zones, running from north to south, each 4.25 metres (14 feet) wide. The living area occupies the whole of the central zone, and from it are openings into all the other rooms. On either side of the living room, there are, to the north, bedrooms. Behind them, on one side, are the shower and lavatory, and on the other is the kitchen/dining room. The building is as open as possible to the north (the shady side) and entirely closed on the south side. Along the south wall runs a continuous zone of cupboard space, and there are also walls of cupboards built into the spaces between the bedrooms and the auxiliary areas. By providing this ample storage, the architects have enabled the clients to keep the rest of the space free of clutter.

Exterior cladding is in black poplar, the same timber used for the tobacco-storage building that the house has replaced (agriculture in the Vega has shifted in the last century from linen, hemp and sugarbeet to asparagus, tobacco and vegetables). The only treatment this wood has received is against parasite attack. It should therefore age and fade naturally.

With the exception of one window, every opening in the outside of the building is a door, making it possible to enter any room directly. On the northern façade, sliding doors run the full width of the living space, and there are also doors opening into the bedrooms. At the back of the building, a skylight illuminates the servant spaces. The openings are framed in natural-coloured metal, and this palette of timber with a little metal extends to the interior, including the built-in furniture. The timber also extends beyond the boundary of the building into a series of decks at different levels on the northern and western sides, providing a link between the rectangular box of the structure and the nearby countryside. Tall, slender trees have been preserved in the building's surroundings, providing a pleasing vertical contrast with the low volume of the house.

Unlikely to distract the attention of visitors who approach with their eyes fixed on the more showy attractions of Granada itself, this little house is nevertheless an extremely satisfactory piece of architecture – an example of architects rising to the challenge of restrictions to create something so spare and rigorously considered that it is hard to see how it could be bettered.

THIS PAGE

TOP LEFT The kitchen/dining room is on the more enclosed, southern side of the house.

ABOVE The shower and lavatory are as uncluttered as every other element of the building.

OPPOSITE

TOP LEFT Section showing the simplicity of the arrangement, and the careful consideration that has been employed.

TOP RIGHT Timber has been used extensively, internally as well as externally.

BOTTOM The central living room runs the full depth of the house.

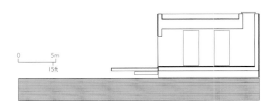

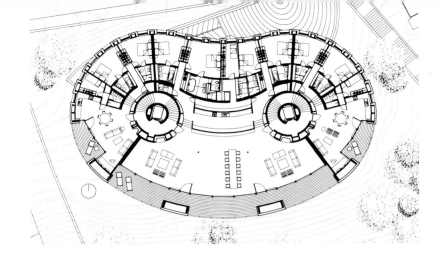

It looks rather as if a space ship has landed in the glitzy skiing resort of St Moritz – but a space ship that is not entirely alien, that in some indefinable way belongs. This is the effect of the Chesa Futura apartment building, designed by Foster and Partners, which combines an unusual rounded form that could only have been created by the latest computer technology with traditional construction techniques applied to locally sourced materials.

Foster and Partners established an international reputation as the epitome of high-tech style through a series of beautifully conceived and executed, if sometimes slightly mechanistic, buildings. This definition lost its sharpness as the architects embraced ubiquitous environmental issues and, at the same time, some of their straight lines and sharp angles softened into curves – but, nevertheless, timber is not a material immediately associated with the practice. Foster and Partners have used timber before, notably for a house in Corsica, completed in 1993, for the deputy mayor of Nîmes, Jean Bosquet, but the architect's signature materials remain steel and glass.

Indeed, it is on such steel-and-glass buildings that Foster have developed their use of parametric modelling, a 3D modelling process that allows the designer to specify or capture the geometric relationship between design features. The parameters that control those relationships can be modified to generate new versions of the design almost instantaneously. Having used this technique in the design of the Gateshead Music Centre in the north of England, the Swiss Re office building in London and the headquarters of the Greater London Authority, Foster have now also applied it to a relatively modest apartment building in Switzerland's Engadin valley. All the buildings mentioned here are non-orthogonal, and in all of them Foster have striven to achieve the greatest efficiency of form and performance. Lord Foster has written, 'The rapidity with which alterations can be made to a design generates a degree of creative freedom, allowing options to be worked up, assessed and improved upon in an organic fashion, providing important lessons along the way.' This approach also gives more authority to the architect, allowing a detailed dialogue between the architect, engineers and cost consultants, and at the same time drawing the contractor and the construction process into relatively early-stage discussions.

At St Moritz, the method has been used to create a flexible building of between six and 12 apartments that make the most of their orientation in terms both of views and environmental

performance, as well as exploiting the envelope determined by the planning regulations. The slightly alien nature of the structure seems appropriate in St Moritz, a resort whose native population is swollen tenfold at the height of the skiing season, mostly by rich foreigners. For some, the place is the epitome of glamour, but the more cynical *Rough Guide to Switzerland* says that it 'sticks out like a sore thumb. Seemingly plopped down unceremoniously amidst the quiet villages of the Engadin – although, of course, it was here long before they were, a spa as far back as the Bronze Age – St Moritz is a brassy, in-your-face reminder of the world beyond the high valley walls, the kind of place that gives money a bad name.'

St Moritz is densely built, and Foster's first concern was to create a building that could sit within the urban envelope, rather than sprawling out into the surrounding countryside – so the apartment block is lifted up on eight pilotis. This classic modernist move ensures that all the apartments have views and follows a Swiss tradition of protecting wooden buildings from prolonged contact with moisture from long-lying snow.

Planning required that at no point should the building be more than 15.5 metres (51 feet) above ground –

a complex constraint, given the sloping nature of the site, and one that the curved form exploits better than a rectilinear building would have done. Similarly, the curves reduce the apparent bulk, which is important since, by effectively eliminating the first two floors, the architect was obliged to make the three accommodation floors larger.

The accommodation consists of a frame of prefabricated glue-laminated beams and a skin of plywood sheets. The malleability of wood makes it easier to achieve the building's doubly curved shape. Since timber is a renewable material, it has good environmental credentials and, by sourcing the material locally, the architect was able to minimize the transport costs and fuel consumption. Compared with steel or concrete, the elements are relatively small and light, making them easier to bring in on narrow mountain roads.

Two concrete cores housing the lift shafts and stairwells provide further stability. This superstructure sits on a lightweight steel structure, supported on the eight sloping steel pilotis. The foundations consist of a sunken concrete box, which houses the plant rooms, car parking and storage spaces. Wherever possible, the architect has used prefabrication, since the winter holiday season restricted construction to eight months a year.

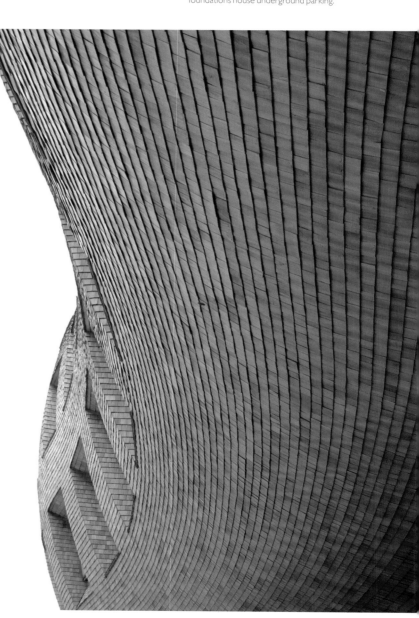

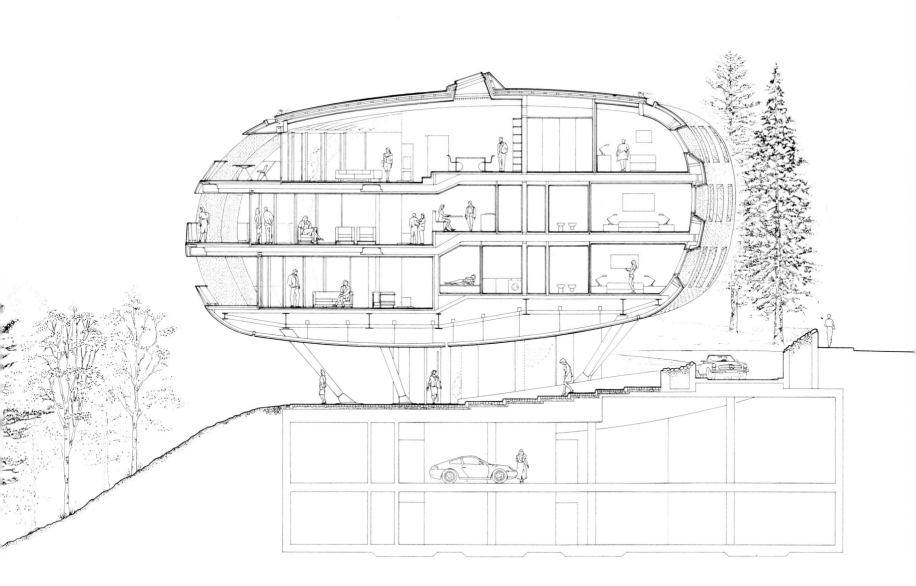

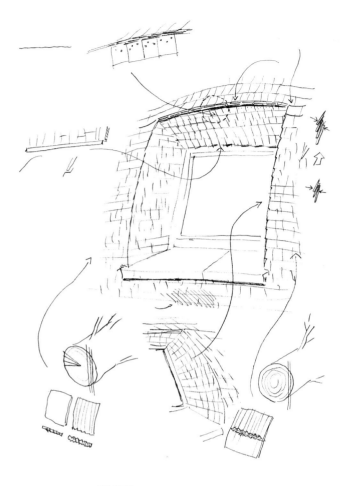

By wrapping the windows around this curved form, the architect was also able to take maximum advantage of the panoramas of the town and the lake. The building stands to the north of the town, so that balconies are on the southern side, giving good views and letting in sunlight. On the north, which faces the mountains and the bleakest weather, the windows are small openings in the walls, which have an insulation-containing cavity 40 cm (16 inches) wide. Picking up a traditional Engadin design detail, the window surrounds are chamfered to allow in the maximum amount of light.

The building is clad in larch shingles, which weather and change colour with time. A traditional material, larch helps the building to blend in with its surroundings. A local family who has practised the craft for generations cut the shingles by hand. Cutting them both laterally and radially made the most efficient use of the material, so that only 80 trees were needed to provide the required 240 cubic metres (8,470 cubic feet) of shingles. The water-draining characteristics of one cut complement the structural strength of the other, and provide a variegated appearance.

By using trees that grow at the same altitude as the finished building, and cutting them in the winter when the wood is dry and contains no sap, it could be guaranteed that the shingles would not shrink. They were applied by hand, using nails, and have a life expectancy of 80 years. The roof is made from copper, another traditional local material. It is malleable enough to be formed on site, even in low winter temperatures.

The apartments have their bedrooms against the highly insulated northern façade, with living areas to the south, where they benefit from the sunlight and the views. Bathrooms and kitchens are in the middle section of the building, where there is less daylight. A building with walls that curve in two directions poses a challenge for the interior designer. There is no storage against the external walls, only on the internal partitions, which radiate from the cores.

The occupants of these apartments will doubtless find them delightful, and there is no denying that the architect has taken its environmental duty seriously. But whether this relatively small building will have much influence on construction in popular winter resorts is less certain, if only because such a distinctive form rarely bears repetition within a densely planned town.

OPPOSITE
At the Mason's Bend
Community Center
in Alabama, USA,
cypress planks were
not bought
readymade, but were
cut down and milled by
the students from
Rural Studio, who built
the project on a
very tight budget.

Architecture thrives on constraints — and the most difficult projects are often those where the architect has an entirely free hand and doesn't really know where to start. That is the problem of designing in a place with no cultural context. Think of the soulless housing that springs up on the outer edges of so many great cities or, worse, of the retail warehouses and out-of-town shopping centres that receive little public attention because they are not even considered to be places appropriate for 'architecture'.

It was in exactly this type of degraded environment that Spanish practice Roberto Ercilla y Miguel Ángel Campo designed a house on the outskirts of the Basque capital, Vitoria (see page 96). Rather than pretending to find inspiration in some ill-considered, recently built housing or opting for pastiche, they decided to draw on industrial design, since the house is in one of the most industrialized parts of Spain. From that decision, and from the client's specific requirements, the design ideas flowed freely to produce a building of beauty and practicality, although very unlike what might have been expected.

Another Spanish architectural practice, Nieto y Sobejano, faced a very different problem in Madrid, where, rather than too much freedom, there was hardly any freedom at all (see page 92). The

form, the volume and the roof of an undistinguished house had to remain, although the client was eager for something modern and special. Cleverly, the architect achieved this by wrapping the house in a new coat to change the external appearance and, internally, by building a new spine to support the opening up of spaces that the client wanted. As with the Vitoria project, clever thinking was required to respond to such a distinctive site.

Quintáns Raya Crespo Architects faced the opposite problem when designing swimming pools for the province of La Coruña in Spain. The brief was to design a prototype that could then be built in a number of small towns, each in a different context. The flexibility and intelligence of the approach is demonstrated in the first built example, in the town of Puentedeume, where the architect managed to incorporate an old stone wall and a protected walnut tree, without compromising the integrity of its design.

Avoiding the imposition of a design signature on a project involves another kind of pragmatism. This was the approach of Peter Hübner in designing a school in Germany's Ruhr valley (see page 78). Since the ethos of the design was that students and parents should be involved as much as possible in the specification and construction of the

buildings, the last thing Hübner wanted was to impose from above the dead hand of uniformity. So, although his work creates a strong skeleton for development, this relates to organization and materials, not to a recognizable aesthetic. Unlike those masterplanners who pay lip service to the concept of design diversity, yet make a plan so unyielding that their involvement will always dominate, Hübner is keen that, visually at least, his contribution should fade into the background. Timber played a dominant role in the construction of the school, partly for environmental reasons but also because it is a flexible material that can adapt to a range of uses and forms.

Such flexibility is demonstrated at Willoughby Barn in Missouri, USA, where the client, despairing of finding a new construction that suited her needs at a price she could afford, bought an old frame and had it transported and re-erected (see page 100). The architect, El Dorado, then created a modern building around the old frame, making extensive use of recycled timber.

Part of the driving force behind Willoughby Barn was the client's restricted budget, but this restriction was as nothing to that experienced by the Rural Studio in Alabama (see page 106). This university-based practice, founded by the late Samuel Mockbee,

employs students to design houses and community buildings for some of the most deprived people in the western world. Given the minimal budgets, materials are not so much recycled as scavenged, resulting in buildings that are unconventional in appearance, but satisfy the needs of their clients. Whether some clients would prefer a more anonymous form of architecture has not been addressed amid the plaudits that the practice has received, but the close working relationship between the architecture students and their clients should ensure that the latter feel positive about the buildings by the time they are complete.

The concept of constructing buildings from waste materials was taken to extremes in the Tower of Babel, built by the Artists' Community of Ruigoord, Netherlands, to mark the new millennium. Intended to be as much a protest as a structure, this must have been one of the few inhabited buildings in which timber's propensity to burn was seen as an advantage: on the night of the millennium, its residents deliberately burnt it down.

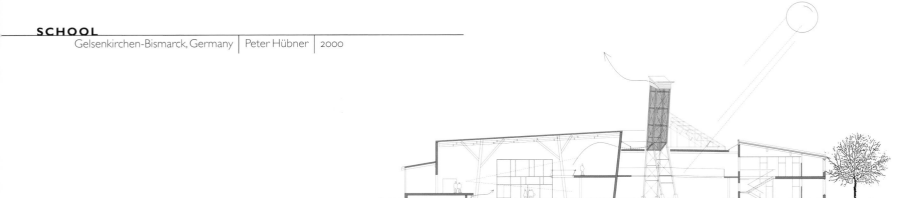

OPPOSITE

TOP   Section showing how the thermal chimneys help to
ventilate the largest spaces, augmenting cooling
through underground pipes and the stack effect in
the internal street.

BOTTOM   The library, at one end of the street, is surrounded
by a pond.

THIS PAGE

ABOVE   Rather than having a single, dominating vision, the
architect has aimed for a mix of approaches that
creates a village-like atmosphere.

TOP RIGHT   Wherever possible, natural daylight is used in the
buildings.

The new school at Gelsenkirchen-Bismarck, in Germany's Ruhr valley, does not, at first glance, have a strongly identifiable architectural style. But, if architect Peter Hübner had had his way, the agglomeration of buildings around a central street would have been even more diverse. Hübner wanted a different architect to design each building, and it was only his client's insistence that this would be too complex to administer that convinced Hübner to compromise. Instead, he achieved diversity by allocating individual buildings to different members of his associated practice, the enigmatically named plus +.

This was not because Hübner wanted to abdicate responsibility or because he lacked a strong agenda of his own. Indeed, a glance through his portfolio reveals a remarkable continuity. In schools and community buildings, he has concentrated on the use of timber, frequently in almost marquee-like structures. He has progressed from a somewhat over-expressive use of the material in such projects as a young people's centre in Stuttgart in 1984 to a more rationalist, though still creative, approach in a school sports hall in Oberhambach in 1994. Hübner's environmental approach is also reflected in the prevalence of planted roofs. Equally important is the involvement of clients and users in the process of design and construction.

At Gelsenkirchen-Bismarck, Hübner has produced his most radical vision yet. He won a competition to create an environmental school in a problem area with a solution that addressed not only the building fabric, but also the organization of the school itself and the learning that went on there. Hübner was keen that the strong architectural vision should not be seen as resulting in a deadening uniformity of appearance and approach – hence his desire to involve other architects wherever possible.

The need for something special was driven by the problems of the area and by the vision of Fritz Sundermeier, an educationalist associated with the local Protestant church organization. Gelsenkirchen-Bismarck is a former industrial suburb that grew up around a large coal mine at the end of the nineteenth century. In the 1960s, Turkish immigrant workers replaced the German workers. When the mine closed in the 1980s, the children of the Turkish workers were left stranded in an area of high unemployment. Since many of them did not read or write German, their prospects were bleak. Sundermeier and the Evangelische Kirche von Westfalen proposed the creation of a multicultural school for 1,100 students. Taking in large numbers of Turkish Muslim children and Catholics, it would carve its place in

THIS PAGE

ABOVE   Forming two-thirds of a circle, the workshop terminates the progression through the main set of buildings.

LEFT   Buildings are constructed with lightweight timber frames, and untreated Douglas fir is widely used for cladding.

OPPOSITE

TOP LEFT   Plan: 1. entrance, 2. cafeteria, 3. library, 4. theatre, 5. central 'street', 6. classroom block, 7. workshop

TOP RIGHT   Colours may appear charmingly random, but, in fact, a colour consultant was used to draw up the palette.

BOTTOM   Green roofs, which are popular in Germany, form part of the environmental mix.

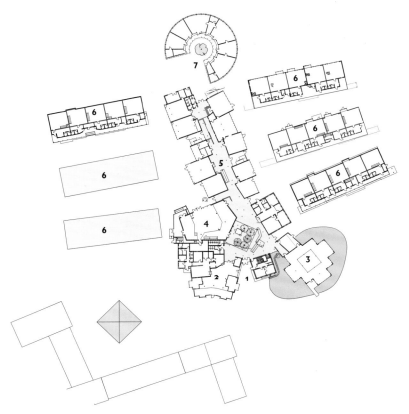

the community through its ecological initiatives, acting as a centre for the community, as well as for its pupils. The school was to be built on a former meadow near its predecessor, allowing a gradual transfer from the old building to the new. Also associated with the scheme was a considerable amount of self-build housing.

Hübner won the competition with the most holistic and radical of all the submissions. The main buildings cluster around an irregular internal street, a space whose form is determined by the shapes of the other buildings rather than carefully planned in itself. Just inside the entrance, there are a cafeteria on the left and the library, set within a pool, on

the right, with music rooms and a chapel above. Next come a theatre on the left and a more prosaic administration centre on the right, then a relatively small number of classrooms including four buildings for special classes, named 'chemist', 'cinema', 'laboratory' and 'studio'. Beyond the end of the street is a workshop in a building that occupies two-thirds of a circle. Farther away from the street is a sports hall.

Flanking the central row of buildings are the classroom blocks. These are being built gradually, to reflect the rate at which pupils are scheduled to move from the existing school – and the pupils have had a lot of involvement in the design. Along with their teachers and

OPPOSITE
The timber 'trees' in the theatre are rotated, relative to each other, in a deliberate attempt to increase the sense of randomness.

THIS PAGE
ABOVE   The library doubles as a church.
TOP LEFT   There are plenty of informal spaces within the school complex.
TOP RIGHT   Children have been involved in the development of the classrooms in which they study.

parents, they have worked with the architects on the planning, modelling and construction, being involved from the conceptual stages to the end, when they applied coats of paint. This means that the blocks vary, but are all based on a lightweight timber frame with a mixture of single- and double-storey accommodation providing a varied roofline. Natural daylight is used wherever possible and, with high levels of insulation and appropriate window sizes, natural ventilation is possible.

The three most complex structures are the workshop, the library/church and the theatre. All are made solely of timber. 'We try not to use steel if we build with wood,' says the architect. Douglas fir, grown in the Black Forest, is used widely, but in the theatre the architect turned to laminated timber because of the requirement to achieve 30 minutes' fire resistance.

The theatre space needs to be as flexible as possible, and, at first, gives a curiously random impression. It is irregular in shape and the roof is supported by timber 'trees', their trunks hexagonal and comprising six individual pieces of timber with a hollow core. 'Branches' emerge from these trunks at a variety of heights. In fact, the trees are identical, simply rotated at different angles – but this was against the architect's wishes, a uniformity imposed

by the engineer for ease of calculation. According to Hübner, 'The theatre is a game with geometrics. In a room with five angles, four trees support a roof of triangles, which create six angles and six branches.'

The large volumes of the theatre and the sports hall mean that natural ventilation would have been inadequate. The architect, working with its environmental consultant Transsolar, has used sophisticated passive ventilation techniques that, in the case of the theatre, also make use of the internal street. These include a combination of thermal chimneys and drawing in of air through underground pipes. Where Douglas fir is used for cladding, it is left untreated and in its natural colour, but elsewhere in the complex a wide range of colours is used. Creating a lively atmosphere, these are certainly not random. Indeed, the project used a dedicated colour consultant.

Hübner is convinced that this building – carefully thought out but leaving space for others to use their initiative – can create a positive environment for education in this deprived suburb. Experience has taught us to be cynical about the power of good buildings to bring about social regeneration, but few solutions have been as carefully considered as this one. It certainly deserves to succeed.

THIS PAGE

TOP RIGHT   Although, in fact, fairly near to the centre of Amsterdam, Ruigoord feels remote in its flat, wet setting.

RIGHT   The building was extraordinarily reminiscent of old paintings of the Tower of Babel.

BELOW   Occupants made an endless series of small accretions to the building, which gave it the stamp of individual personalities.

OPPOSITE

Using discarded wooden pallets for construction introduced a degree of uniformity.

Cultural Freeport Ruigoord and the Artists' Colony of Ruigoord are two of the names given to a community based on a boggy island in the Netherlands. Created in 1973, at the height of the hippy era, it has stubbornly continued to exist, its closest parallels perhaps being the houseboat dwellers of Amsterdam and the Danish enclave of Christiania – the type of 'alternative' living to which these conventional northern European societies seem uniquely tolerant.

The impression given by the romantic image of Ruigoord is that it is somewhere very remote. This is impossible, of course, in the Netherlands, Europe's most densely populated country. In fact, Ruigoord is a kind of suburb of Amsterdam, and easily accessible on the 82 bus from the city centre. A lot of the activity in Ruigoord is linked to performance, through the Amsterdam Balloon Company, and its manifesto says, 'Nation has made war on nation, but artists from different cultures have kept on cooperating and inspiring each other. It is for this spirit, on the interface between ancient traditions and avant-garde experiment, that Ruigoord stands open. Empower the Imagination, now especially, at the beginning of an as yet unformed new era.'

One of the most dramatic and complex events at Ruigoord was the decision, in 1999, to construct a Tower of Babel. This

THIS PAGE

LEFT Residents and friends of the Artists' Community of Ruigoord celebrated the Millennium evening with a huge party.

BELOW The burning of the Tower of Babel was the centrepiece of the celebrations.

OPPOSITE Partying continued as the structure burnt to the ground.

was a reaction to the news that the enclave was under threat of redevelopment by international companies for industrial use.

Timber is a forgiving material, ideal for constructing a building without real plans. The community members sought donations from local firms, which, ironically, provided waste materials – in the form of hundreds of old timber pallets – from exactly the sort of industrial enterprise that the inhabitants of Ruigoord reject. Forming the basis of the structure, the pallets impose some material consistency that other seemingly random accretions could not obliterate. In fact, the finished structure, with its gently sloping, spiralling external ramp, bore a remarkable resemblance to the paintings of Pieter Breughel and Abel Grimmer. Most of the timber was unpainted, with decoration coming from the occasional coloured door, from banners and hanging mobiles, from a whimsical cantilevered birdcage, and from two items essential to modern communications: a postbox and a large sign bearing the address of the community's website.

Inside, the tower provided living and working quarters for the community's artists. This pragmatic, seemingly random, arrangement carried an echo, on a smaller and less threatening scale, of Hong Kong's former forbidden city, which, though confusing, also had its own logic and organization. In one way, the Tower of Babel resembled the most commercially rigorous of construction projects – it had a very tight and unmovable deadline for completion. It had to be finished by the last day of 1999, in time for an enormous party on the site, which culminated in the burning of the tower. Can this sort of dramatic gesture have any effect? Logic would say no, but four years after the tower was constructed, in reaction to the imminent threat to the community, Ruigoord is still there, still thriving and still organizing events.

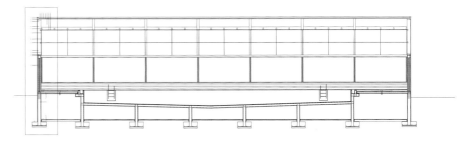

OPPOSITE

TOP   The long section shows that the pool building is a simple, but well illuminated, box.

LEFT   The architect has dealt with the horizontal nature of the building by adopting a stratified approach to materials: concrete up to a certain level, with timber above.

RIGHT   There are large windows, with slender mullions, on the northern side of the swimming pool.

THIS PAGE

ABOVE   The simple approach to design should allow similar pools to sit comfortably in a number of different locations.

RIGHT   A long courtyard running between the back of the pool enclosure and the auxiliary building lets light come in to both.

Swimming pools are popular places, although they can be somewhat brutal, with noise echoing off hard surfaces to make a swim more of an ordeal than a refreshment. And, despite their popularity, pools rarely make money – operators of health clubs often treat them as 'loss leaders', attracting customers for more profitable activities.

For local authorities, therefore, pools can be a liability. The province of A Coruña in northwest Spain tackled the issue by trying to make it more controllable. Recognizing the need for a reproducible form of pool that could be adapted to local needs, it launched a competition to design just that. Local practice Quintáns Raya Crespo

Architects (since re-formed as VIER arquitectos) won the competition, and built its first example of such a pool in the town of Puentedeume.

This was a real design challenge, since the site was restricted and two elements had to be kept: a stone wall and a walnut tree. But the architects' concept – which consists of housing the pool itself in a rectangular box and putting all associated services in a building enclosed by a concrete wall – worked superbly. The pool building is oriented so that the windows that run the length of its north side look out past lawns and trees to the estuary of the River Eume. On the southern side, light can filter in through slender

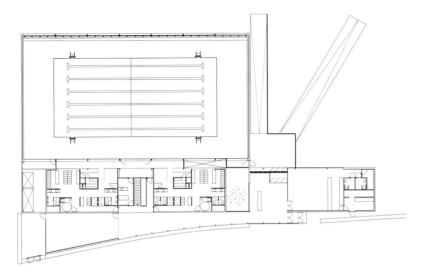

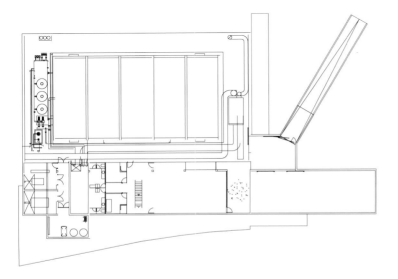

courts between the pool building and the service building. Another court, at right angles to the pool building, surrounds the walnut tree. The stone wall has been incorporated into the building's enclosure.

The architect has dealt with the horizontal nature of the building by adopting a stratified approach to materials. Concrete is used for the auxiliary building and the base of the pool building. Above this, on the pool building, is the glazing, with widely spaced and slender mullions. Above again is a timber superstructure with horizontal timber cladding. The superstructure is a post-and-beam construction of glulam elements, 1.4 metres (4 feet) deep, with the beams spanning 20 metres (66 feet) across the width of the pool hall. With some wind-bracing as well, these posts and beams form the skeleton onto which the cladding – consisting of pine, treated in an autoclave – is fixed. On the eastern face, the cladding is fixed to notches, cut into the superstructure, in a pattern that allows light to filter in.

This concept of enclosure within a timber box is continued internally, with walls and ceiling covered in laminated timber panels, treated to resist humid atmospheres. The modular nature of the structure made it possible to fix all the panels without any need for on-site cutting. Timber, again treated pine, is also used for the floor surrounding the pool. The boards, which are grooved for slip resistance, are laid with gaps between them, to accommodate any swelling and also to let water drain away between them; this is essential because they are level with the surface of the pool.

Puentedeume's pool hall is, therefore, a much gentler and more welcoming environment than many comparable buildings, and the careful consideration given by the architect to the use of materials means that the complex sits comfortably in Puentedeume, and should do so equally in other towns where the design is destined to be built.

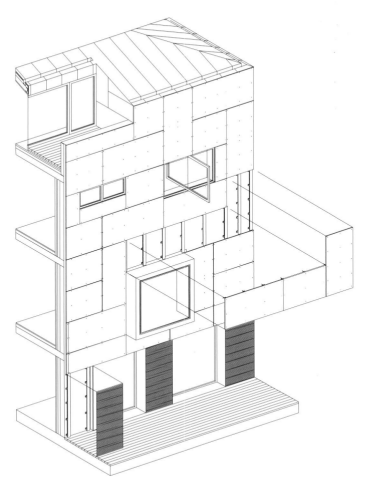

LEFT — Deep reveals to the windows are one attractive result of the overcladding.

TOP RIGHT — Careful consideration was given to the sizes and orientation of the bakelized boards.

BOTTOM RIGHT — Boarded strips run up to the front door, which sits within the lower zone of cladding in aluminium.

THIS PAGE

ABOVE LEFT — Anatomy of a facelift: the new façade was fixed to the existing one to satisfy both planning restrictions and the client's desires.

ABOVE RIGHT — There is a pleasingly abstract arrangement of fenestration.

If some projects represent an architect's or a client's dream, a house in Chamartín, Madrid, came closer to being a nightmare. How does an architect give a client the modern and spacious house desired when byelaws appear to make it impossible? That was the problem faced by architects Fuensanta Nieto and Enrique Sobejano. Based in Madrid, the pair have an impressive portfolio of work in their home country and abroad, most of it on a larger scale than this house, and a great deal of it arts-based – but it is unlikely that they have faced a bigger challenge.

The client's house was in a pleasant street of buildings with little architectural distinction – to which their own house, constructed in the 1950s, was no exception. Since the house is set on a relatively generous plot, designing a replacement would have been a fairly straightforward challenge. However, byelaws prohibited demolition and required that the original building materials and volume be retained. Another requirement was that the house should keep a pitched roof, sloping in all four directions.

Even now, some civil servant may be toiling away to close a loophole in the byelaws that the architects exploited, since what they have done is to comply with the letter, but most definitely not with the spirit, of the law. They have kept the existing materials and walls of the house, but they have enclosed them in a new skin, so that the house looks completely different. Internally, they have built a spinal structure containing services and storage that has allowed them to create considerably more open floors than existed originally. In both cases, this new work makes extensive use of wood.

Aluminium battens fix the new façade to the existing exterior walls, leaving an air space between them so that the effect is of a ventilated façade. At the lowest level, this new façade is of undulating aluminium, but on the rest of the building it is of high-density bakelized boards. Bakelizing is a treatment with a resin that is cooked at about 150°C (302°F), to create a hard, impermeable surface. Commonly applied to specialist papers, it is also used on plywood, for applications such as formwork and advertising boards, where it is necessary to withstand repeated abrasion. On the house, the top layer is of elondo wood. Visually, the effect is attractive – a rich, reddish brown colour that varies slightly across the surface. The architect has carefully worked out the pattern of application, with some boards in portrait and others in landscape format, to fit in with the pleasing geometry of the windows. The effect, in a warm monotone, is almost like an abstract painting. The double

façade means that windows have attractively deep internal sills. Externally, the use of timber continues with a boarded strip to the front door. The pitched roof is in copper, to harmonize with the colour of the overcladding.

The new spine, built of boxwood, houses everything from ducting and a pantry to bookshelves and wardrobes, and runs across almost the entire width of the building. There is also an elegant timber staircase in ash, the timber also used for the floorboards. Both these allow the house to have the open, clear spaces that the owners wanted, but with the warmth of a natural material and without banishing personal possessions in an over-rigorous obsession with order.

This house was, in a sense, an unnecessary project, an example of the ridiculous hoops through which architects are sometimes forced to jump. Perhaps in the distant future an archaeologist will examine this house within a house, and wonder why it was wrapped up in this extraordinary way. It may be difficult to understand the planning foibles of the late twentieth and early twenty-first centuries, but they have certainly led the architect to produce a highly imaginative result.

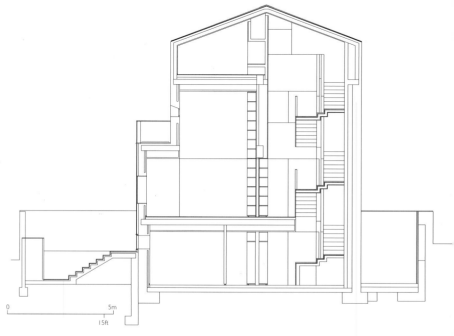

0   5m
15ft

HOUSE

San Prudencio Uleta, Vitoria, Spain | Roberto Ercilla y Miguel Ángel Campo | 2002

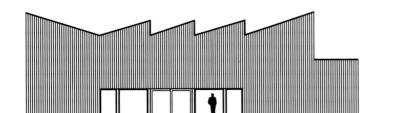
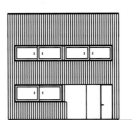

OPPOSITE

TOP The stern façades offer few opportunities for inquisitive visitors to look in.

BOTTOM Locally sourced red cedar planks clad the building.

THIS PAGE

RIGHT Sun loungers put outside on a sunny day provide one of the few hints at habitation.

BELOW Model showing the sawtooth form of the roof that draws light into the heart of the building.

How can you create a sense of context in a region of ill-conceived and ill-controlled growth? This is a question that architects Roberto Ercilla y Miguel Ángel Campo tackled at San Prudencio Uleta, outside the Basque capital of Vitoria. Vitoria has one of the highest standards of living in Spain, resulting in a lot of poorly planned luxury housing on its outskirts. Dream homes have been created with little regard for their surroundings or the history of their location.

One home-owner who has thought about context is the owner of this house, not far from the city boundaries – and the chosen context is not what one would immediately have expected.

The building sits on the edge of an industrial park – the Basque country being, after all, one of the most heavily industrialized regions of Spain – and follows an industrial aesthetic that suits the client's particular needs. The architects, who come from Vitoria but have worked all over Spain, had previously used laminated timber in the construction of an uncompromising and uncompromisingly modern hotel building in a formless wasteland at the edge of Irun, on the French border. At San Prudencio Uleta, they have used such timber to create a building that provides exactly what the client needs, while making few concessions to traditional ideas of prettiness or domesticity.

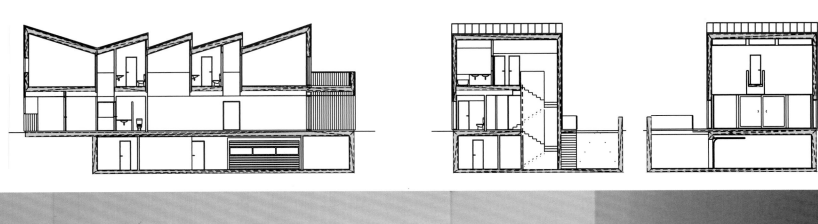

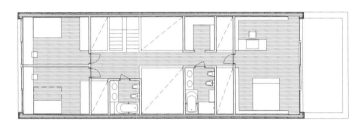

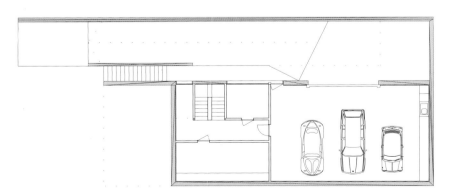

What the client wanted most in the house were light and privacy – apparently incompatible until you think of bringing in light from the roof. What better approach can there be than the sawtooth roof, beloved of those throwing up deep-plan and relatively inexpensive industrial space? At the house in San Prudencio Uleta, this guiding principle has resulted in a design with relatively few windows, and none leading into private areas. Instead, light streams in from the roof and is carried down into the central living space. The upper-floor bedrooms lead off a central corridor, but there are double-height spaces on either side that enable light to find routes down to the ground floor, where it is disseminated through the open-plan layout.

Structurally, the building is of reinforced concrete, but it is clad outside with local red cedar planks supported on pine battens. Both have received the same treatment to ensure durability. Timber used internally has been painted white to reflect the light. The effect on the visitor is uncompromising and faintly hostile – of a timber box that gives little away about the occupants or the purpose of the building. Only on sunny days, when sun loungers appear on the strictly rectilinear patio, is there a sense that this could be a building used for pleasure.

This is a house that recalls not only the industrial aesthetic, but also the artist's studio, the courtyard houses of southern Spain and the Arab world, and certain Japanese houses that turn their backs resolutely on the street to celebrate their own internal life. Beyond the toughness of the external timber planking there is a sense of luxury and privilege. And, even though this imaginative design seems to exclude the outside world, it also integrates better with its environment than most of its more extrovert neighbours.

WILLOUGHBY DESIGN BARN
Weston, Missouri, USA | El Dorado | 2001

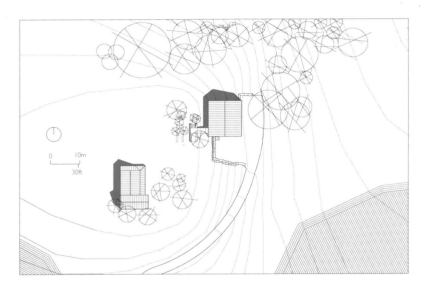

THIS PAGE

TOP RIGHT The new barn sits on a sloping site.
ABOVE Site plan.
BOTTOM RIGHT The simple appearance, particularly as night falls, gives little indication of the sophistication in choice of materials or uses.

OPPOSITE
Cladding is in corrugated copper and corrugated fibreglass.

OVERLEAF
LEFT By not heating the main spaces, the architect was able to leave the frame exposed, without fear of it warping.
RIGHT The wood flooring was reclaimed from a former gymnasium.

Barn conversions are more common these days than the construction of entirely new barns, so it is exciting when a new barn is built – although this strikingly contemporary-looking building in Weston, Missouri, is not all it seems. The Willoughby Design Barn is not strictly a new building, nor is it entirely a barn. It is an ornament to its location and a testament to the ingenuity and dedication of a client and architect, who possessed more imagination than cash.

The client, graphic designer Ann Willoughby, wanted a 'barn' with an agricultural purpose that would also serve as an extension to her 1880s farmhouse, even though not physically connected to it. With her architect, Dan Maginn of El Dorado, based in Kansas City, Willoughby initially talked to local

carpenters and was disappointed by the conventional nature of the solutions they offered. But on a visit to Red Barn Farm, a nearby demonstration farm with traditional buildings, she saw a model of a timber-framed barn and was told that a similar, full-sized structure was about to be dismantled and turned into floor planks. Willoughby bought it and had it reconstructed at her farm on a new concrete foundation. The pine frame is a no-nonsense, elegantly proportioned, structure that the architect took as the starting point for the rest of the design and choice of materials.

Set on sloping ground (the house is at the high point, with commanding views), the new barn is largely workmanlike on the ground floor, with one side dedicated to farm storage and the other to car parking. A central timber staircase leads to the upper floor, which is designed as a place for Willoughby's clients and colleagues to visit – and stay, since she is a long way from a major urban centre. The space on one side of the stair is designated for entertainment and includes a dining table. Reflecting the changes in external level, there is an entrance on this side. The other side is described as a studio and has a sleeping loft above it, reached by a suitably agricultural-looking ladder. There is also a bathroom on the studio side, an enclosed room that is the only heated space; this may seem a spartan

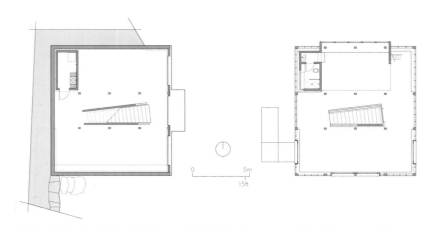

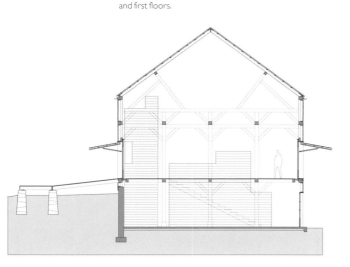

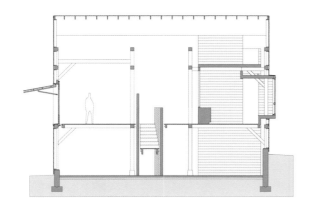

approach, but few visitors are likely to make the journey in a harsh Midwestern winter. The decision not to heat the rest of the space has made it possible for the frame to remain exposed, in conditions similar to those experienced in the first century of its life, thereby avoiding the drying-out problems that heating could cause. The architect has treated the frame with enormous respect, as an almost sculptural object. None of the new walls and openings – kept to a minimum – abuts the frame, so it maintains its independence.

Timber is used extensively on the interior. As with the frame, much of this is reclaimed. The wood flooring had its first life in a gymnasium, and the panelling is reclaimed pine siding that was flood-damaged in 1933. Cedar and glass were used for the sliding barn doors, and window openings are also framed in wood.

Although Willoughby Design Barn is a relatively small project, it is among the larger projects carried out by this particular architect. Founded in 1995, El Dorado is as much involved in the process of making as in design, and has its own workshop. Indeed, a great deal of its early work concerned the making of furniture. On this project, it acted as general contractor and carried out the internal cabinetwork, also making the handles for the main doors, plus handrails and metal brackets.

If all this suggests a worthy, but rather retro, Arts and Crafts approach, that couldn't be farther from the truth. Internally, there is a clear, austere geometry, and the external appearance is both crisp and surprising. The architect originally planned to clad the building in galvanized iron, but then it learnt that it would cost only another $12,000 (around £8,000) for 16-ounce corrugated copper. This material has been used with the corrugations running horizontally and kept exposed on the inside of the building. Coupled with the use of corrugated fibreglass for glazing set in the walls and the roof, this creates a sense of restrained, appropriate warmth and luxury – all the more impressive when one learns that the entire project cost only $62.50 per square foot (around £400 a square metre).

MASON'S BEND COMMUNITY CENTER 2000

OPPOSITE

TOP Old car windscreens form the glazing of the community centre.

BOTTOM Students cut down cypress trees and milled them into planks to form the laminated beams.

THIS PAGE

ABOVE Although relatively small, the community centre forms an important meeting place for the 150 people who live at Mason's Bend.

TOP RIGHT Materials may be salvaged or very cheap, but the result is professional and impressive.

The latter half of the twentieth century demonstrated, through the ingenuity of engineering solutions, that timber can be a sophisticated and finely finished material. But there are circumstances in which its simple flexibility, its usability and reusability are much more important. Pre-eminent in this is the work of Rural Studio from Auburn University, Alabama.

There is no single distinct style to be found in this work since it is produced by successive groups of students. But there is an underlying ethos, established by the founders of Rural Studio, professors Dennis K. Ruth and Samuel Mockbee, the public face of the venture, who died at the end of 2001. Universities are always places of privilege, but rarely so glaringly as at Auburn, which is in Hale County, Alabama. This is the area immortalized by writer James Agee and photographer Walker Evans in the book *Let Us Now Praise Famous Men*, based on their stay there in 1936. Compassionate, engaged and angry, the book details a level of rural poverty that is almost unimaginable in the western world. Nearly 70 years later, improvements have been far fewer than might have been hoped. In 1999, average per capita income was only $12,661, and unemployment was about twice the national average.

In response to this situation, Mockbee and Ruth set up a programme for their architecture students that would involve them in designing and constructing houses and communal buildings for some of the most needy members of the community, working in both Hale County and adjacent Perry County. Described as 'context-based learning', it has a set of well-defined objectives:

- To give students of the School of Architecture the opportunity to learn the critical skills of planning, designing, and building in a concrete, practical, and socially responsible manner.
- To form leadership qualities in students by instilling the social ethics of professionalism, volunteerism, individual responsibility, and community service.
- To help communities, through partnerships with the state and local welfare agencies, provide suitable and dignified housing.
- To develop materials, methods, and technologies that will house the rural poor in dignity and mitigate the effects of poverty upon rural living conditions.

There are three distinct programmes of work, one for second-year students to build one-off houses, one for fifth-year students to create community buildings, and one for students from elsewhere. The results have been economic, practical and surprisingly architecturally imaginative. Obliged to scavenge, scrounge or buy materials cheaply, the

ANTIOCH BAPTIST CHURCH 2002

LEFT   Aluminium covers most of the exterior of the church.

BELOW LEFT   The opportunity to install a baptismal font (foreground) was one of the major reasons for having a new building.

BELOW   Although most of the materials were salvaged from the existing church, the effect is entirely contemporary.

BOTTOM   Joists, panelling and floorboards were among the salvaged materials.

HERO CHILDREN'S CENTER 1999

RIGHT The barn-like buildings are clad in coloured timber planking and have tin roofs.

BELOW The covered passage joining the buildings doubles as a waiting area.

students have built structures that vary from the sophisticated shack to works reminiscent of the early creations of Frank Gehry. Given the hot and humid climate, many of the structures are not entirely enclosed, since the provision of shelter is often enough. Much of the work takes place at a base in Newbern, where students have built their own accommodation and workspaces over time, using scavenged and experimental materials, including, most recently, cardboard clippings. Indeed, the students consider no material too humble, having even built one house almost entirely from recycled carpet tiles.

Even where materials appear relatively sophisticated, there has been significant input from the students. For example, a community centre at Mason's Bend has a central meeting space created from a sloping framework of laminated timber beams. But these were not bought readymade. Instead, the students cut down cypress trees and milled them into planks to create the laminated beams. Cypress was also used to create benches in the space. Neither of these elements is 'rough-hewn', but each has an elegant simplicity. The low, enclosing walls are of rammed earth, with a rusting metal drip on top. The sloping beams support a metal-framed canopy that is partly clad in aluminium sheet and partly in what seems an unusual, but attractive, glazing system – in fact, it is

made from the windscreens of 1980s General Motor Company sedan cars, salvaged from a Chicago scrapyard. Serving a multitude of functions, from a place of worship to a centre for childcare, this building also has an important symbolic one in a location where the 150 residents, comprising four extended families, live in trailer homes or very basic, decaying houses.

Whereas at Mason's Bend the salvaged material came from a distant city, the Antioch Baptist Church cannibalized an existing building. The previous church was no longer viable because of foundation problems, and lacked both a lavatory and a baptismal font. Having decided to construct a new building, the students salvaged everything they could from the old one – roof and floor joists, pine heartwood wall panelling, tongued-and-grooved boards and exterior corrugated metal. More than three-quarters of the materials in the new building come from its predecessor, but the building itself is entirely different in form. The interior is almost all of timber, with a long horizontal window offering views of the graveyard. However, this inner structure is protected from the elements by an outer wrapping, a cranked structure supported by handbuilt, composite wood-and-metal trusses and covered in aluminium. Only at one end does the inner timber box protrude.

SHILES HOUSE 2002

TOP LEFT Oak shingles that clad the house were cut from old shipping pallets.

LEFT Car tyres, clad in a cement render, support the timber staircase.

STUDENT HOUSING 1999

TOP RIGHT Students design their own housing and studios, using them as an opportunity to experiment with materials.

ABOVE Interiors are designed as much for practicality as for style.

PERRY LAKES PARK PAVILION 2002

RIGHT The pavilion roof is described as a 'dancing plane'.
BELOW Slender metal uprights support the cedar roof structure.

The student project at Greensboro in Hale County also fulfilled an urgent need. The HERO Children's Center is an addition to the Hale County Empowerment and Revitalization (HERO) Family Resource Center. It offers a place for various authorities to interview and counsel children who have been abused physically, mentally or sexually. Before it was built, these interviews had to take place in Tuscaloosa, one hour's journey away.

Serving a variety of complex functions, including the provision of an interview and observation room, with a one-way window disguised as a mirror, the construction is visually simple, consisting of a group of low, barn-like structures, clad in painted timber planking, with tin roofs. These buildings are joined by a loftier covered passage, which can serve as a waiting area. Supported by telegraph poles, with some rudimentary cross bracing, the passage has a pitched roof of paired timber members, covered in corrugated metal and perspex. This central walkway leads to a playground, with an enticing central play structure, again constructed from telegraph poles and smaller timber elements.

Second-year students also made use of telegraph poles for the Shiles House, lifting it above the wet ground. Much of the superstructure of this house is of timber, including a lattice supporting the roof, but where the building descends to ground level the structure consists of old car tyres. The tyres, clad in a cement render, also form the support for a central timber staircase. The exterior of the building is clad in oak shingles, cut from wooden shipping pallets.

Perhaps the most elegant of the students' projects is one of the simplest: a pavilion at Perry Lakes Park in Perry County. The park was closed to the public in 1974 when fish were stolen from the nearby US Southeastern Fish Cultural Laboratory. Following the closure of the laboratory in 1994, and with considerable local effort, the park reopened in 2001. The students designed the pavilion on the site of an old picnic spot at Barton's Beach, building it almost entirely from donated cedar, which they themselves cut down and took to be milled in Greensboro. Open on three sides, the pavilion has slender metal uprights supporting the cedar roof, which is described as 'a dancing plane' and rises slightly erratically from each set of supports until it reaches a height of 7 metres (23 feet) at the front. The cedar floor curves up to provide benches. Like all Rural Studio's buildings, the pavilion serves a multitude of functions: as a place for community gatherings, catfish fries, family reunions, and as an outdoor classroom for Judson College.

OPPOSITE
International superstar
Frank Gehry used
timber extensively in
the Maggie's Centre
for cancer treatment
in Dundee, Scotland,
which won the Royal
Fine Art Commission's
British Building of the
Year Award in 2004.

Buildings are increasingly used to define places. Since Frank Gehry designed the Guggenheim Museum in Bilbao, other cities have striven to achieve the 'Bilbao' effect, to create an architectural icon that can define and regenerate a whole city. Interestingly, Gehry, famed for his use of advanced computer technology and of space-age materials, such as the titanium cladding in Bilbao, turned to timber for the roof of his much smaller Maggie's Centre, the therapeutic healing facility that is his first building in the UK.

Whereas for Gehry timber only became an option when he was working on a more intimate scale, Santiago Calatrava – another architect whose buildings seem made to adorn postage stamps – used it on a far more extrovert scale on his wine production plant in the Rioja region of Spain (see page 126). More likely, in fact, to appear on a wine label than on a stamp, this building is an icon that will come to represent the wines of the producers and attract visitors from a distance.

The transport buildings shown here work much more directly in their own place. The Vancouver station is designed primarily to attract travellers to what, for them, is a new form of transport, but also, like the Aix-en-Provence TGV station, to form a core for the development of a new district (see pages 114 and 132). Both these buildings are crucial parts of the planning jigsaw and set high standards of design that, it is hoped, will be followed in succeeding buildings. The reconstruction of Hounslow East station, in a much more mature setting, aims to restore some of the local pride originally engendered by the more iconic West London underground stations and, at the most basic level, make the station more accessible (see page 118). Its historical inspiration is expressed in a design that is forward-looking and inventive.

Thomas Herzog's building for the Hanover Expo site was also intended as a centrepiece for other developments, but in an interesting historical context (see page 136). It was one of the defining structures of the original Expo, and the only one to remain. Once the initial show had been dismantled, it had a new role to play in future development of the site – a building with more presence than any legacy building since, arguably, Paris's Eiffel Tower.

If Herzog's structure was a geographic centre for a set of temporary exhibition structures, then von Gerkan, Marg + Partner have created that crucial sense of place for their permanent sister, the normally soulless exhibition centre. Like all the buildings in this chapter, the Rimini Fiera (see page 140) uses timber in part to give a human scale and some warmth to buildings that, through their need to be iconic, can too often seem cold and inhuman.

Smallest of the projects in this section, the View Silo House in the wide, open spaces of Montana (see page 122) shows that a landmark building is sometimes more in sympathy with a place than a building that tries unsuccessfully to disappear. Although it will be seen by far fewer people than the other buildings in this chapter, View Silo is a reminder that architects have to accept the responsibility of placemaking, even in remote locations.

BRENTWOOD SKYTRAIN STATION

Vancouver, Canada | Busby + Associates | 2002

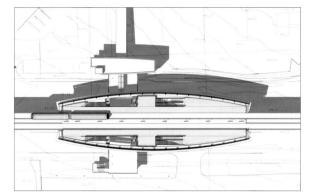

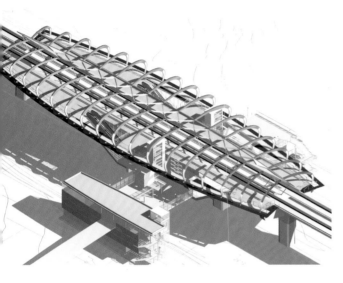

How to persuade commuters to abandon their cars is a problem facing most developed and developing cities. Everybody agrees that it is essential to reduce gridlock and improve urban air quality, but many car-drivers are resistant to change and reluctant to give up the freedom they associate with their vehicles. Some cities, such as London, which successfully introduced congestion charging at the start of 2003, favour the use of a stick. Others prefer the carrot. Vancouver, on Canada's west coast, is in the latter category.

With its great advantages of scenery and climate, Vancouver is determined to prevent uncontrolled suburban sprawl by concentrating development on a network of planned new centres. Although these centres are linked by a road, the Lougheed Highway, the city authority wants commuters to switch to more sustainable methods of transport than cars. It has therefore constructed the 13-station Millennium Line, the second line of its electrically powered Skytrain system, an elevated metro. Lifted above the road traffic, and providing panoramic views of city architecture and the surrounding mountains from front and rear carriages, Skytrain offers a pleasurable travelling experience. But how can passengers be persuaded to try it?

Part of the answer lies in station design. The Vancouver Rapid Transit Project

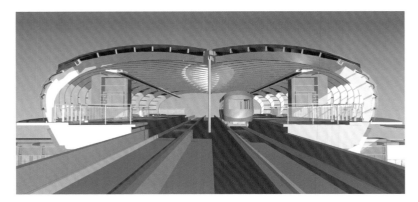

Office appointed local architect Busby + Associates to design two stations. The more dramatic is at Brentwood, which is intended to serve as the catalyst of a new town centre. The architect's solution – faintly reminiscent of a woodlouse, or some similar insect, squatting across the elevated railway lines – has translucent sides so that it can act as a beacon at night. Passengers approach the station by a new bridge straddling the main road, but running beneath the railway lines. From there, they take a lift or escalator to what turns out to be a simple, but elegant, shelter, made less formidable and more welcoming by the use of timber. The canopies over each platform are supported by curved, tapering glulam beams, set into tall, white-painted metal shoes, which rise from the concrete structure of the railway itself. This use of a curved glulam-and-timber roof is reminiscent of a station (albeit a temporary one) built in Rome by the architect Marco Tamino. Only 300 metres (980 feet) from St Peter's, the station was the terminus of a new metro line that provided access to celebrations to mark the new millennium.

The Brentwood station is wider in the centre than at the ends, to accommodate the lifts and escalators, so the canopies bulge out, curving in the horizontal, as well as in the vertical, plane. Flat glass in seven facets rises up around the concave curves of the sides, with all but its highest members covering the steel shoes. From outside, the dominant materials are steel and glass, but from the platforms the observer is far more aware of the glulam beams and of the curved-timber roof decks they support. This roof is made up from 50 × 100 mm (2 × 4 inch) softwood elements, nailed together in the centre. The two timber canopies meet only at the very ends, but there is steel cross bracing across the elliptical opening to provide seismic stability. Entirely practical in origin, the bracing adds the finishing touch to a drama that should surely tempt commuters away from their dreary cars on a road that offers neither views nor speed.

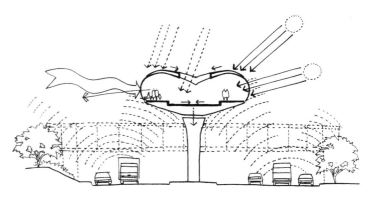

UNDERGROUND STATION

Hounslow East, London | Acanthus Lawrence & Wrightson | 2001

Constructed in the early 1930s, the western section of London Underground's Piccadilly Line has some of the most architecturally distinguished stations on the network, including architect Charles Holden's designs for Southgate, Arnos Grove and Sudbury Town. The station at Hounslow East, however, had no such distinction. On a line that has become far more important since it was extended to Heathrow airport, Hounslow East is one of the last above-ground stations before the railway assumes its proper underground character on the way to central London.

The original station was nothing much to look at and access was difficult. It was set on an embankment, the continuation of a bridge over an adjacent cross road. Reaching the westbound platform after buying a ticket involved going out of the station, under a bridge and up the embankment. As well as being a less than satisfactory experience for passengers, the necessity for this procedure made it difficult to ensure that every passenger had bought a ticket before boarding a train.

When architects Acanthus Lawrence & Wrightson won a competitive tender to redesign the station, their answer sorted out the circulation with two new structures, one on either side of the embankment. The first to be built, and the more important, was on

THIS PAGE

LEFT   Pre-patinated copper was used so that the roof would look green immediately.

BELOW   The canted roof covers both the entrance and the station platform.

OPPOSITE

LEFT   Structure of the diagrid roof.

RIGHT   The support system for the roof.

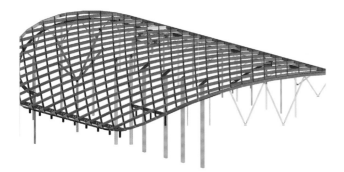

the west side and incorporated a ground-level ticket hall and ancillary accommodation. A stair and lift give access to the platform, which had to remain at its old, high level. A tunnel under the tracks leads to another set of stairs and a lift up to the other platform. The ticket office has a rounded shape that pays homage to the designs of Charles Holden. The station's palette of materials sets it apart from the mundane brick suburban houses nearby, but its swooping copper-covered roof brings it down on one side to the scale of the surrounding buildings. On the other side, at its full height, it provides shelter for passengers on the platform.

Timber has traditionally been used as a material for above-ground London tube stations, but at Hounslow East it is used on the roof in a novel and inventive manner. The architect worked with engineer Buro Happold and with Cowley Structural Timberworks, the UK's foremost expert in timber construction, to develop a two-way-spanning diagrid roof – a roof formed of relatively short elements, spanning in two directions. These make a grid of near squares, with a leg projecting from each corner of the square. An internal timber 'tree', consisting of oak struts emanating from a steel 'trunk', supports the roof in the centre. At the edges, it rests on the external walls.

This is not the classical environment in which lamella structures are used, since the approach is not used here, as is more common, to create an arched structure. Timber lamella structures were patented by Friedrich Zollinger in 1921, and were used commonly and successfully between the two world wars. Steel versions have been used – on the Houston Astrodome in 1965, for example – but have never proved widely popular. The two main advantages of lamellar construction are that regular elements can be used to form almost any shape, and that the relatively small elements are easy to handle on site.

At Hounslow, the roof is a constant barrel vault with a radius of 23.8 metres (78 feet). The design team selected a 1.25 metre (4 foot) grid, with each individual lamella being 2.5 metres (8 feet) long. The lamellas are identical, except that half are mirror images of the others, so there were no specials apart from wall plates and edge beams. The material used is a laminated veneer lumber (LVL), in this case made from Finnish softwood. It is dimensionally stable and can be supplied in large sizes, up to 40 × 1.8 metres (131 × 6 feet).

There are two main versions. In the one used for the lamella structure, the strands are oriented in the same direction. The other version, which has a cross-ply formation, was used for the roof decking, which was 27 mm (1 inch) thick, and tongued and grooved. This decking stiffens the structure and, to make proper contact with the lamella structure, the lamellas needed to twist slightly. Cowley Structural Timberworks, working with Buro Happold, developed a solution to make this possible. Each lamella is offset slightly at its junction with a cross member, and the edges of the lamellas are planed, so that the decking always lies flush to the top edge of the lamella and the wall plates on the bottom.

Since the timber structure was to be exposed internally, the connections had to be visually acceptable, as well as effective. Bolting is the traditional method of fixing, but this would have looked clumsy on such a relatively small structure. Instead, a special connector was used. This consists of a long, threaded bolt sleeve, glued into one end of a lamella. A threaded receiving tube went in the other end. On site, the bolts were threaded through a drilled hole in the cross member into the end of the next lamella in line, and the joint tightened up at an access hole in the side of the lamella. Crucial to the connection's success is a coupler embedded within the transverse beam. Normally, there are two of these bolts in each end but, where the shear forces demanded it, this number could be

increased to three. The offset angle between the lamellas, which was needed to allow the deck to lie flat, was achieved by offsetting slightly from the vertical the two connectors in the ends of the lamellas. Steel stanchions support the edges of the roof in most places, but where the edge of the roof cantilevers over the platform it is supported on triangulated timber struts that sit on specially shaped steel stanchion tops.

Above the deck of LVL, there is waterproofing, then a vapour barrier, insulation, battens, a ply skin and, finally, the handsome copper roof. Pre-patinated sheets, which had already acquired the characteristic green colour of an aged copper roof, were laid across the ply skin and joined by a combination of traditional and modern methods. The roof was rolled over the edge and a metre or so back under the eaves. Secret gutters, bull-nose eaves and soffits in copper contribute to the roof's continuous appearance. A translucent cladding material on the street elevation allows daylight to enter the ticket hall, ensuring that passengers can benefit fully from their last taste of natural light before plunging into the tunnels of the underground system.

VIEW SILO HOUSE
Livingston, Montana, USA | RoTo Architects | 2001

THIS PAGE
The tower draws on imagery of grain silos and, looking as if it is twisting in the wind, is a suitably tough structure for its rugged environment.

OPPOSITE

LEFT   Sections through the building show how the architect has made maximum use of its twisted geometry.

RIGHT   True vertical elements are clad vertically with cedar slats, reclaimed from pickling barrels.

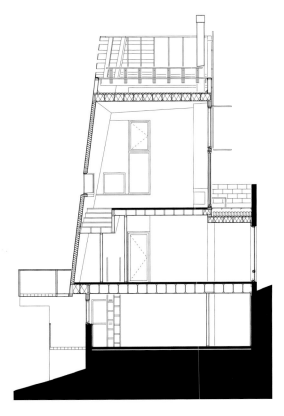

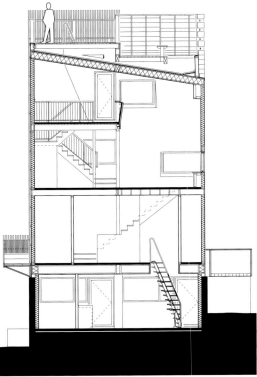

The mere name Paradise Valley is enough to make one yearn to live there – and for those who love wide-ranging views and a sense of space, Paradise Valley in Montana doesn't disappoint. Just north of Yellowstone Park, in what has become known as Marlboro Country, it offers warm summers and mild winters, dramatic storms and views of the Absaroka and Gallatin mountain ranges, made more spectacular by an absence of trees. Los Angeles-based RoTo Architects had a client, Ron Gompertz, who, after five years away from the valley, found the lure of the landscape too strong to resist and asked the practice to design him a house that, for the time being at least, would be a part-time residence.

The site, near Livingston at the north of the valley, covers 5.5 hectares (14 acres), with only one feature that offers any shelter at all – a bank of the Yellowstone River, which has now receded from this area. Gompertz was keen that part of the building should give him the opportunity to climb up and enjoy wide-ranging views. In response, the architect designed a house in two parts, only one of which has been built. Set into the ridge, the house consists of a tower (built) and a low-lying building that wraps around it (a future project). As well as satisfying the client's requirement for views, the rationale was that a dramatic tower would be more in sympathy with the qualities of the landscape than a medium-height,

blocky building. Drawing on the area's grain silos and elevators for inspiration, the tower is less obtrusive than a lower mass would have been. It has an asymmetric, twisted form, giving it a dynamic tension that suggests it is being distorted by the wind.

Entrance is at the southwest corner to the lowest level, which is partially set into the hillside. Two bedrooms and a bathroom occupy this space. A stair leads up to the next floor, where there is an office and living room. Over the living area is a mezzanine with space for cooking and eating. Above that, the staircase, now open to the elements, continues up to a viewing platform.

Although some masonry is used in the building, there is also extensive use of timber, both internally and externally. All of the window frames are timber, as is the construction of the mezzanine, which has a slatted timber railing – an effect repeated on the outside of the building. Whereas much of the cladding

is horizontal timber, on the south and west side there are elements projecting at true verticals from the main volume, which tapers upwards. These elements are clad with 2 x 2 cedar slats, reclaimed from barrels used for pickling. They are spaced between 1 and 6 cm (0.5 and 2 ½ inches) apart, and stand about 5 cm (2 inches) proud of a waterproofing layer. This layer consists of asphalt-roll roofing in bright red. The reclaimed timber is itself in a variety of colours, ranging from a silver-grey to a dark purple that is almost black. Set in front of the waterproofing, this creates a depth of colour and an effect that changes with the angle of view.

If constructed, the next phase of the building will be a low mass to the south of the silo. But the first phase is a fine structure in its own right, offering the client the views that he craves, while also acting as a handsome object in the landscape for other lovers of the region, whether they are observing from a distance or simply passing by.

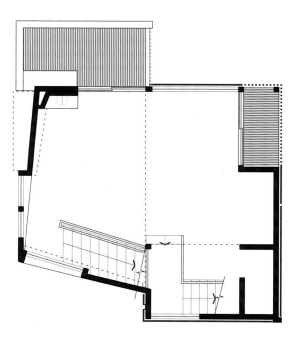

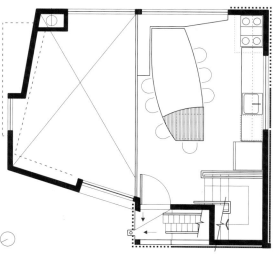

OPPOSITE

LEFT   Living room, with the mezzanine above.

RIGHT   Plans of the mezzanine floor (below), which
        contains the kitchen and dining areas, and of the top
        level, with its viewing platform.

THIS PAGE

LEFT   A certain amount of masonry mixes with the
        timber cladding.

BELOW   Entrance is at the lowest level, partially buried in the
        hillside, which also incorporates bedrooms and a
        bathroom.

BODEGAS YSIOS

Laguardia, Spain | Santiago Calatrava | 2001

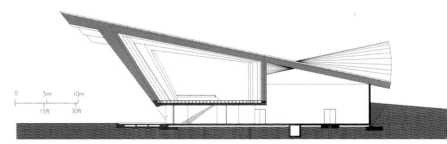

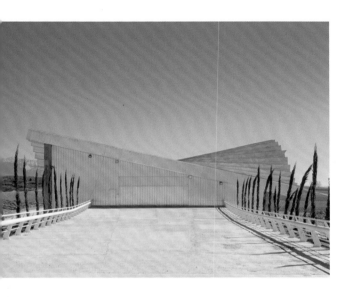

OPPOSITE

TOP   Section from front to back of the winery, showing that straight elements are used to create the undulating curves.

BOTTOM   The front façade is clad in strips of cedar, echoing the colour of the soil.

THIS PAGE

ABOVE   The short-side façades are treated in a much more workaday manner, clad with corrugated metal.

RIGHT   The central wave of seven rises to a higher peak.

Buildings can help to create a brand, and for a new winemaker in Spain, the Bodegas & Bebidas group, there seemed no better way to take advantage of this idea than to employ the country's most flamboyant architect-cum-engineer, Santiago Calatrava. With its new Bodegas Ysios in the Rioja region, the winemaker has ended up with a building that both serves its functional purposes and provides a great draw for visitors. Already featuring prominently on the company's website, the building is also sure to make an appearance on the wine labels.

Founded in 1998, Bodegas Ysios is near Laguardia, northwest of the Rioja capital of Logroño and at the foot of the Cantabrian mountain range. Climatically important for the quality of the wine, Rioja Alavesa, the mountains also provided inspiration for the form of the building. Eschewing his love affair with the zoomorphic form, Calatrava has instead designed a structure with a series of curving roofs. Faced with the constraints imposed by the building's function and a relatively limited budget, the architect continued his exploration of how to create curved structures using straight elements – a challenge that has fascinated him for years. Laminated beams of Scandinavian fir span nearly 26 metres (85 feet) from the front to the back of the building, rising and falling in a pattern that gives drama to the interior as well as the exterior.

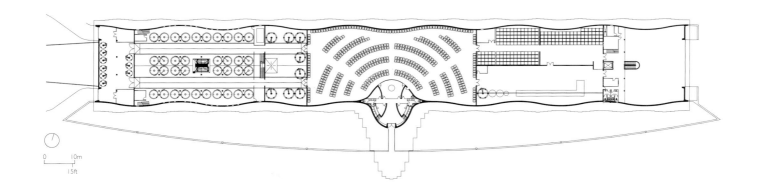

0   10m
15ft

OPPOSITE

TOP Plan of the building, through which the wine-making process progresses from left to right.

BELOW The undulating roof echoes the form of the Cantabrian mountain range.

THIS PAGE

RIGHT The back of the building, visible from the vineyards, is in raw concrete.

RIGHT THIS PAGE
The visitor entrance is at the dead centre.

BELOW The extraordinary geometry also makes for
exciting spaces internally, with the laminated beams
of Scandinavian fir exposed.

OPPOSITE
Visitors are entertained on the upper floor at the
centre of the building, from where they can enjoy
magnificent views.

The building is 196 metres (643 feet) long, with a main entrance facing south towards the main road and the mountains set dramatically behind it. It has load-bearing concrete walls that undulate on both the front and back façades. This undulation adds stability to the long walls. Keeping the curves synchronized on the two walls means that the distance between them remains constant. Where the walls bulge outwards most, they are at their highest; where they are most concave, they are at their lowest. Since the most concave element on the front will be matched by the most convex at the rear, and vice versa, this means that the beams spanning from front to back are at constantly changing angles. Hence, with one simple geometric concept, the architecture has generated drama in three dimensions.

For a working winemaker, this would probably be enough, but the building also has a grand axial entrance for visitors. The central element, the middle wave of seven, pokes up 10 metres (32 feet) higher than the rest to accommodate a dining and seating area for visitors, with a glazed wall offering dramatic views over the plains to the hilltop town of Laguardia. By projecting forward, this gesture also allows the insertion of a visitors' lobby, without interfering with the linear production processes. These are straightforward.

Grapes (up to 1 million kilograms/ 2.2 million pounds per harvest) come in at the western end, and move through production and barrel-cleaning areas to storage in the central area, and then on to bottling, bottle storage and shipping. Finished bottles of wine leave the building on the eastern side.

The small east and western façades are simply clad in corrugated metal, as if this were almost any industrial shed. In contrast, the 'public' south façade is clad in strips of cedar, in a conscious echo of the colour of the soil. The back of the building, visible to those working in the vineyards, is raw concrete, and the roof is clad in reflective aluminium. 'The effect of sunlight on the roof creates a wave-like movement, like the changes in tonalities of the surrounding vineyards,' says Calatrava. It is fortunate that these vineyards are at too low a level for the people working in them to be dazzled by reflections from the roof on days of remorseless sunshine.

Bodegas Ysios is growing tempranillo grapes on 65 hectares (176 acres) and takes its winemaking as seriously as its architectural commission. Repeat business will depend on the quality and price of the product. But for those visiting the region, Calatrava's building will doubtless prove an attraction. There can be few better three-dimensional advertisements.

RAILWAY STATION

 Aix-en-Provence, France | AREP | 2001

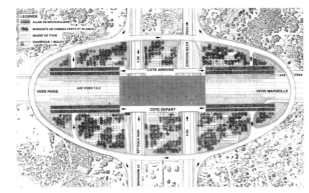

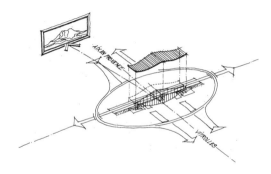

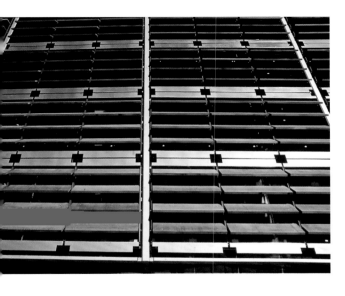

OPPOSITE

TOP   The TGV station is intended to form the
          centrepiece for new development.

BOTTOM   The screen of untreated cedar louvres on the
          western façade is controlled automatically to
          provide shade from the sun.

THIS PAGE

TOP LEFT   Views of Mont Sainte-Victoire were central to the
           architect's concept for the station.

TOP RIGHT The station, seen from the west, with Mont Sainte-
           Victoire behind it.

ABOVE   The cedar louvres are arranged in rows of four,
           with strips of solid aluminium between them.

France has been a world leader in fast, efficient rail travel, with its network of TGV trains setting the standard. The first of these lines was built between Paris and Lyons, in the centre of the country, and this line has now been extended to Marseilles, the country's second city. Journey times between Paris and Marseilles can now be as short as three hours. This line, like other TGV lines, was built relatively easily for three reasons. The French countryside is fairly lightly populated; the development that accompanies a TGV line is seen as beneficial; and the planning system is able to force through new projects. As a result, TGV trains run on new, straight tracks, and this means that they frequently need new stations outside the city centres.

The extension of the TGV line south has led to the construction of three such stations, at Valence, Avignon and Aix-en-Provence. This last station, the most southerly of the three, is actually midway between Aix and Marseilles, and within easy reach of Marseilles airport. All three stations were built under the direction of Jean-Marie Duthilleul of AREP (Aménagement Recherche Pôles d'échanges), the station development arm of SNCF, the national railway.

Working with landscape architect Desvigne & Dalnoky, Duthilleul decided that each station should respond to its context, rather than following a unified pattern. This may seem common sense, but it represented a departure from established practice. Previously, each line had its own identity, echoed in the unified design of its stations. A precedent had, however, been set by Santiago Calatrava's show-stopping station at Lyons-Satolas airport. A similar change in approach was also evident in London, where the newest underground line, the Jubilee Line extension, designed in the 1990s, broke away from a previously unified approach by employing a different architect to design each station. On the TGV line, the decision was also influenced by the fact that the stations were set in 'nowhere places', where they might well form the catalyst for new development, and therefore it was essential that they should have distinct local identities.

Some unifying characteristics are evident, however. The hot summers in the south of France make it necessary to provide protection from the heat and dazzle of the sun. At the Aix-en-Provence station, the station structure provides shade to the ground-level track and platforms. It has a curving roof that peaks in the middle, supported on chunky glulam columns of untreated iroko, spaced to echo the carriage lengths of the trains, from which rise angled steel struts. The eastern side of the station is open, offering views to

Mont Sainte-Victoire, the local landmark, made famous in the paintings of Paul Cézanne, a native of Aix.

Mont Sainte-Victoire has a distinctive, symmetric, almost Japanese form, and this is eerily echoed in the appearance of the western façade of the station. Blocking one's view of the mountain, the station seems almost to replace it. The western side is enclosed by a double glass wall that curves outwards, and in front of it is a screen of untreated red cedar louvres coming down to a few metres above ground level. These smallish louvres, crisply detailed in bands four deep, on an aluminium framework and with solid aluminium set between them, respond to the sunlight, shutting to keep out the hot afternoon sun and, with the glass façade, providing shelter from the biting Mistral wind.

The station is surrounded by a sea of car parks, above which the wooden 'mountain' appears to float. Once some trees have grown, it will seem more directly set in a landscape. Reflecting the French tradition of formal planting, their position and significance have been calculated precisely by the landscape architect; in this case, each station has been addressed in a similar manner, although with some local differences. At Aix, plantings of thyme, myrtle and santolina will provide some of the evocative smell of the garrigue.

Twin avenues of planes trees, the traditional companions of French country roads, will delineate the approaches to the stations. Rows of cypress trees will provide station windbreaks, and the parking areas will be both shaded and softened by 'orchards' of local trees (in Valence and Avignon) and by holm and white oaks in Aix-en-Provence. These are also being used to mark the outline of future development – something that is likely to happen, given the enthusiasm with which the French embrace their new stations, and the care and consideration that has been given to their design and situation.

THIS PAGE

TOP CENTRE   Chunky glulam columns of untreated iroko, spaced at the length of train carriages, support the roof.

BOTTOM LEFT   Timber floors help give an air of calm to the upper waiting area.

ABOVE   Angled steel struts emerge from the top of the columns.

OPPOSITE

TOP LEFT   The form of the roof is reminiscent of Mont Sainte-Victoire.

TOP RIGHT   Trains serve two island platforms.

BOTTOM   Users of the station are protected from the elements, but not isolated from their surroundings.

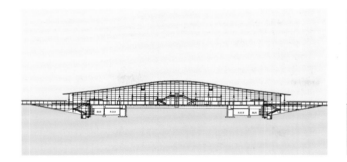
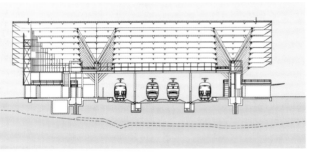

0   500m
1500ft

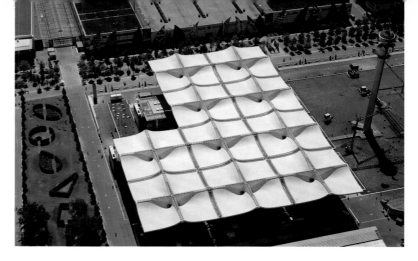

OPPOSITE

TOP   Although its size is impressive, the canopy occupied
           a fairly small proportion of the Expo site.
BOTTOM   Even to the casual observer, this collection of timber
           umbrellas is obviously something special.

THIS PAGE

ABOVE   Plan and elevation of one of the ten units that make
           up the canopy.
TOP RIGHT Above the timber is a synthetic, impermeable
           translucent skin.
BELOW   Concept sketch showing the scheme as a provider
           of shelter.

Professor Thomas Herzog, who is based in Munich, is an architect who has always treated architecture as a form of research. Every one of his relatively modest number of built works pushes technology and thinking forward in a new way. But this is not a cold-hearted embrace of technology. Deeply involved with environmental issues, Herzog is concerned to create true sustainability in his buildings, in terms both of materials and the way that buildings relate to their surroundings.

This is reflected in his canopy at the Hanover Expo, held in 2000. As part of a project that, by its nature, involves a great deal of 'throwaway' structures, Herzog's canopy was the one item always intended to have a permanent life. In a place where the weather is decidedly unpredictable, this massive structure provides protection from both rain and sun – in a manner that allows even the casual observer to understand that timber is being shown off and exploited in entirely new ways.

The L-shaped canopy consists of ten elements (arranged as if two are missing from a four by three rectangular array). Each measures roughly 40 × 40 metres (130 × 130 feet) and is more than 20 metres (66 feet) high. In each, a weighty, square-sided mast supports a wavy square umbrella of latticework on glulam beams. These ten panels are joined together and provide each other with structural stability, minimizing deformation under snow and wind loads.

The analogy with trees is obvious, with the beams curving up out of the trunks at a 'branchlike' angle, and the canopy of smaller elements taking the role of small branches and twigs. But the romanticism of this concept, with the traditional role of trees as shelter, does not tip over into feyness, and it is evident that every element of this ornate structure is working hard and playing a vital role.

The supporting columns comprise four whole, sawn-timber sloping uprights, connected by glulam panels and steel elements, with steel feet anchoring them to a below-ground concrete ring beam. Each of the timber columns is 16 metres (53 feet) long and comes from a single silver fir tree up to 200 years old from the southern Black Forest. Cut in half longitudinally to speed drying, and then joined together again, these trees were selected very carefully, by a combination of observation and ultrasonic testing. The columns may be metaphorical 'trunks', but the real tree trunks are used, counter-intuitively, upside down, since the stresses are highest at the tops of the columns and so the larger diameter was needed there. The diameter is 95 to 110 cm (37 to 43 inches) at the top and 68 to 74 cm (27 to 29 inches) at the bottom.

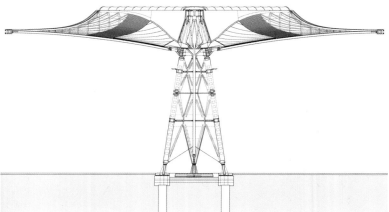

THIS PAGE
Sturdy 'trunks' support an array of branches.

OPPOSITE
The 'ripped shells' of the umbrellas provide interest overhead.

The large size of these trees meant that there was no option but to dry them naturally. After seven months of drying, it was found when construction started that they had not dried as much as expected. This meant that the engineer, IEZ Natterer, had to scale down some predictions of their behaviour.

Triangular frames of glulam, covered with laminated veneer lumber (LVL), 33 mm (1⅓ inches) thick, stabilize the towers. Some steel elements are also included, to prevent horizontal distortion. All the steel connectors that join the timber elements had to be designed specially to take into account the distortion caused by the continued drying of the timber. Bolts had to be accessible for further tightening. A central steel structure at the top of each tower passes down the loads from the cantilevered beams and the umbrella itself – technically termed a 'ripped shell'. These doubled curved shells, and the cantilevered glulam beams that support them, have a very 'natural' form that could only be obtained by the use of the most sophisticated mathematical modelling.

The cantilever beams are 19 metres (62 feet) long and consist of two elements – a lower curved beam that follows the curvature of the ripped shell and an upper straight element. As they move towards the ends of the beams, these two elements come together into a single straight beam. The shells themselves each weigh 36 tonnes (35 tons) – a lot of weight to support on cantilevers above the ground. The form of the ribs that make up the shell is dictated by the design forces, and they are joined by layers of LVL boarding. Most connections are by screws, but gluing was used in the areas under highest stress.

Additional layers of boards above the ribs provide further stability. The umbrella is covered with a synthetic impermeable translucent skin, 5 mm (⅕ inch) above the timber structure, supported by a series of cables. It provides considerable protection from rain, while the gap permits ventilation. The fixing of the membrane is more complex than the simple infill observed from below. In fact, this is the only sleight of hand seen in this building – what looks awe-inspiring but very natural from below has some of its workings concealed above the canopy itself, where few will ever see them.

When dealing with structures of this level of innovation, architects and engineers cannot rely on their gut instincts. Wind and snow loads were simulated in a wind tunnel and produced unexpected results. With most canopy roofs, the wind load is directed upwards. It turned out that at Hanover this load was directed downwards, providing an additional load on the structure. Design details were worked out carefully, not only to provide structural performance, but also to ensure that the structure was protected from rotting. Construction was also complex, with large prefabricated elements being transported to site as outsize loads, and a considerable amount of pre-assembly taking place under cover, adjacent to the site.

The result is a structure that, while not appearing effortless to construct, looks supremely logical, as well as elegant. It is a virtuoso piece of work, made possible by the fact that it had only to provide one simple function – that of shelter. Serving its purpose admirably at Expo, and still in place, it should have sent some of its visitors away with a renewed appreciation of the potential of timber. As Herzog moves on to his next discovery, we should expect to see some of the lessons learnt at Hanover filtering through into other buildings.

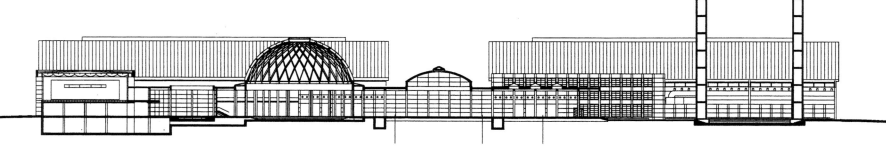

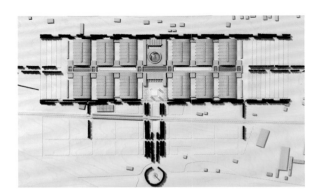

OPPOSITE

TOP   A strongly axial design leads visitors through the centre of the exhibition complex.

BOTTOM   A circular dome, 30 metres (100 feet) across, is one of the main features.

THIS PAGE

ABOVE   The repetitive nature of the halls offered savings in the construction process.

RIGHT   There are echoes of classical architecture, appropriate to Rimini's history.

The thought of going to an exhibition centre makes most people's hearts sink. Important meeting places, where there is a chance to see new things and meet new people, exhibition centres are usually huge and, far too often, soulless, confusing and depressing. They give the impression of being cut off from the normal world, in an artificial and ugly environment of bad ventilation and worse design.

How refreshing, then, to see a new exhibition centre that bucks all these trends by being logically laid out, airy, full of natural light – and which makes generous use of timber, a material not commonly associated with such locations. That is the case at the Nuova Fiera di Rimini, which uses warmth and natural materials to make the exhibition centre a welcoming place to visit and to do business in.

Although Italy hosts the Milan furniture fair and important exhibitions in Bologna, Germany has certainly been the leader in massive fair halls for the last few decades. Now Rimini has decided to catch up. Appropriately, it appointed Hamburg-based architects von Gerkan, Marg + Partner, who had, as part of their distinguished portfolio, designed exhibition halls in cities including Hanover and Düsseldorf.

Rimini is a town that, although commonly associated with cheap-and-

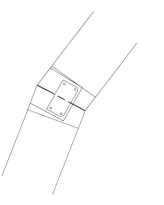

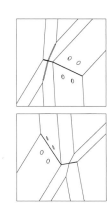

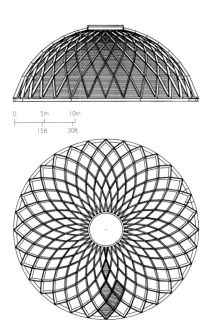

cheerful seaside holidays, has a long and illustrious architectural history. This is reflected in the approach to the fair buildings, which the architect has described as 'orientated around the Emilia-Romagna tradition, which has characterized European architectural history since the ancient world and the Renaissance'. The design is strongly axial but, within the clear geometry, classical elements are interpreted in a contemporary manner.

With an exhibition area of 80,000 square metres (860,000 square feet) and a service area of 50,000 square metres (538,000 square feet), the Fiera consists of 12 exhibition halls, congress and conference rooms, event areas, restaurants, shops, administration offices and auxiliary and storage rooms – quite enough, if the organization were bad, to make it disorientating and overwhelming. To avoid this, the architect created an entrance forecourt with a fountain and four tall, square light towers to signal its presence from a distance. The main entrance has a portico and a circular domed meeting space. The single-storey exhibitor halls are arranged along colonnaded walkways. They are modular to allow maximum flexibility of use, despite the formal layout.

Both the dome roof and the roofs of the exhibition halls are in timber.

The exhibition hall roofs span a 60 × 100 metre (197 × 320 foot) column-free space, a feature that is popular with exhibition organizers. Along their central apex, glazing rises above the timber structure, again bringing light into the space. The architect has used a lamellar structure for the roofs, developed in the 1920s by Friedrich Zollinger. However, by using modern techniques of laminated timber construction, it has managed to produce spans far larger than those Zollinger could achieve. The use of identical, relatively small elements, which are easy to transport, is ideally suited to projects like the Rimini Fiera, where all 12 exhibition halls have the same form.

Each roof consists of lamellar wood, laid in a framework made up of a regular mesh of diagonally placed, rhomboid-shaped elements, measuring 3 × 6 metres (10 × 20 feet). Each beam in this module has the same section, 16 × 70 cm (6 × 28 inches), wherever it is within the roof. At the ends of the roof are arches, also in lamellar wood, with a rectangular section of 50 × 70 cm (20 × 28 inches). Where four beams join, the joints connecting them have to be able to transfer both the bending-axial stress and the shear stress, to ensure that the structure is truly continuous. Specially developed for the project, these joints consist of a steel plate, connected to the four beams by pins

and a central X-shaped element bolted to the plate. The cavities between the steel and the wood are filled with a special grout. Once the assembly is complete, these steel elements are completely invisible.

At 3 metre (10 foot) intervals, the roof is connected via hinges to a steel perimeter box beam, which is supported, in turn, on a concrete substructure. Most of the stability of the roof comes from its vaulted shape and from the way it is restrained at the edges, but there is also a contribution from the planking that clads it, which is fixed from the top by nails. The circular dome uses similar technology. It has a 30 metre (100 foot) diameter and is 22 metres (76 feet) high at the crown. A central oculus brings in light both to the space and to illuminate the dome itself, which has a latticework of structural members coming together towards the apex. Timber boarding behind runs circumferentially.

The architect used Scandinavian timber and took care to ensure it was all from renewable resources. At the opening ceremony, architect Volkwin Marg said that the building was intended to connect the 'past to the future, with references to antique architecture and with a dedication to the culture of this region and of this country, which has survived all the ages. It is an architecture oriented towards an ecological future that distinguishes the greatest and most modern European wood-covered building, a portrait of beauty, technology and respect for the environment.' He described the success of the project in this way: 'The Italians have organized a competition and we have worked with them to create a unique experience: as disciplined as Prussians, hardworking as Swabians, and always punctual, they cost half as much as Germans and are timely in making decisions.'

Another way of looking at this synergy of cultures is that a distinguished German architect has embraced an Italian architectural tradition to build a complex that, by making wise and imaginative use of Scandinavian timber, transcends the usual bland international experience of visiting exhibitions.

OPPOSITE
Savinkin/Kuzmin
exploited the sensuous
properties of plywood
to the full when they
designed the interior
of the Cocon Club
in Moscow.

In the early 1990s, organizations such as DEGW, the London-based architect and space planner, put a lot of effort into analyzing the timescale in which change took place in buildings. DEGW argued that change happened at one speed (the slowest) to the fabric, at another to the services and at a third (the most rapid) to the fixtures and fittings. Since then, the prominence of such thinking has declined. Some of the arguments seem self-evident, while others are too mechanistic for the less formalized approaches to work that we have today.

But it holds true that the interiors of buildings are generally less long-lasting than the exteriors, since fashion, use and ways of working dictate relatively rapid change. This is often reflected in the design: the interior architect can create something specifically for the current needs of the user, rather than having to think too much about flexibility over a long period. Moreover, an interior has to cope only with the depredations of human traffic and not with those of the weather. The interior is therefore an excellent place for experimentation. Designing interiors is also often a way for architectural practices to establish themselves, in that clients seem more willing to trust new practices with the inside of a shop, a bar or even an office than with the structural and planning complexities of a whole building.

Wood has always been a vital part of interiors. It is a traditional material for furniture and floors, and in recent years it has won back a large part of the market from carpet. Tactile and warm both to the touch and the eye, wood makes environments more welcoming. But it can do much more than that.

At the Bally store in Berlin, Craig Bassam has used a high-quality flooring product to cover all surfaces in a sophisticated manner that makes the Swiss company's concerns with quality and detail evident to all customers (see page 150). Since the shop has large windows, Bassam's near-obsessive use of timber manages to avoid the relentless, and rather claustrophobic, impression created in, for example, some traditional Finnish timber houses.

At Renzo Piano's Parco della Musica in Rome, there is an equal level of technical control, but it serves a different end (see page 154). Here timber – American cherry – helps to create the carefully calculated acoustic. The application of timber for its acoustic properties is not restricted to concert halls. For example, at Temple Quay House, a large government office building in Bristol, southwest England, local architect Stride Treglown used slotted timber panels with an acoustic quilt behind them to reduce reverberation within the atrium.

The relative ease of shaping timber, particularly in its engineered forms, makes it suitable for the creation of 'pods', or insertions into large, open spaces, which are becoming popular in offices eager to foster less formal ways of working. Timber has been used in that way in the office of TBWA\Chiat\Day in San Francisco, and also in the UK headquarters of the Danish pharmaceuticals company Lundbeck (see pages 166 and 168). Nor is this idea of inserting a timber object into a large, open space restricted to office buildings. At the Peckham Library in South London, which won its creator, Will Alsop, the UK's most prestigious architectural award in 2000, ellipsoid timber pods are used to house an interview area and an early-learning centre. Working with the superlative craftsman Gordon Cowley, Alsop created these from timber ribs, covered with oriented strand board and with ply-clad triangular elements. Even more expressively, the Russian practice Savinkin/Kuzmin has used plywood in an extraordinarily sensuous way to create the Moscow nightclub Cocon Club. The initiative even extends to a lavatory pod, with a door that opens like a submarine door, suspended high above the rest of the club. The most extraordinary aspect of this project is that, although plywood seems an integral part of the design, it was not the architect's first choice. Originally the architect wanted to clad

the pods with titanium and abandoned the idea only because the necessary technical expertise was not available.

All the projects mentioned above are new constructions, but timber also has an important part to play in heritage buildings. A sympathetic material in that it was generally available at the time when the old buildings were constructed, timber can also be treated as relatively temporary. If you build in concrete, your decision is probably irrevocable; and, while stone and brick masonry constructions may be removable, they are heavy and have an air of permanence. The latest thinking about the conservation and restoration of historic buildings is that all interventions should be reversible. There is an awareness that some of the 'correct' thinking of the past, in terms of restoration, was flawed and that we may be making similar errors today. The only way to avoid this is to ensure that everything that is done can be undone. At the castle of Peñaranda in northern Spain, the architect has created a new use for a hollow stone tower by inserting a timber structure that can simply be taken away again when no longer required (see page 162). In other chapters of this book, we see how timber can be designed for durability and long life; at Peñaranda, it is timber's potential impermanence that makes it such an attractive choice.

BALLY STORE

Berlin, Germany | Craig Bassam Studio | 2001

TOP LEFT   Bally's store on Berlin's elegant Kurfürstendamm was chosen as the flagship for the new design approach.

TOP RIGHT   The warmth and simplicity of the wooden interior act as a magnet for shoppers.

BOTTOM   Oiled light oak was used for floors, walls and ceilings. The stools, based on a Swiss tractor seat, were carved in the Bally factory with the same technology it uses to make its shoe lasts.

THIS PAGE

ABOVE   Clothes are displayed like art objects against the simple background.

RIGHT   White-lacquered cubes form one of the few other elements in the design.

Given that fashion is such a fickle business, it was a great achievement for Swiss shoe company Bally to have stayed at the top of the tree since its foundation in the Swiss hamlet of Schönenwerd in 1851 by Carl Franz Bally. Not surprisingly, when the Texas Pacific Group bought the company in 1999, it decided that the time had come for an updating. The company brought in Scott Fellows as its creative director, who set about brightening the brand, while sticking to some of its traditional strengths. And he appointed Australian architect Craig Bassam (now of Bassam Fellows) to design a new concept retail store in Berlin, as well as a headquarters building in Switzerland.

This was Bassam's first retail project and it shows – not through any incompetence, but in the freshness of his thinking. He turned the 300 square metre (3,230 square foot) store at 219 Kurfürstendamm, Berlin's prime shopping street, into an extraordinarily homogeneous, understated, yet rich, space. Designed to show off the latest lines not only in shoes, but also in accessories and clothes, the store is utterly contemporary, but nevertheless reflects the Swiss craftsmanship and obsession with detail and quality that have always characterized Bally.

Bassam achieved this by using a Swiss-made standard flooring product of fine-grained, oiled light oak throughout – on

THIS PAGE

LEFT   Red-lacquer trays in the cupboards add a touch of
            colour.
RIGHT   Construction by Swiss cabinetmakers ensured a
            beautiful level of finishes.

OPPOSITE

TOP LEFT   Handrails to the stairs, deliberately designed to be
            comfortable to hold, are supported by oxidized
            bronze.
TOP RIGHT   Slightly offsetting the oak planks one above the
            other adds a degree of visual dynamism.
LEFT   There are 300 square metres (3,230 square feet) of
            selling space, on two levels.

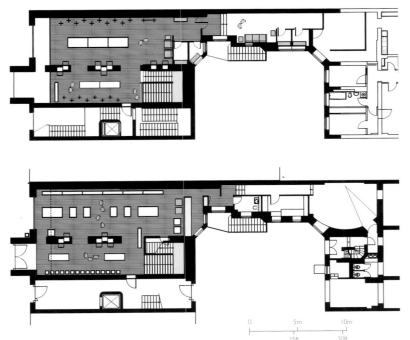

the floors, naturally, but also on walls, ceilings and stairs. The feeling in this two-storey building is of being enclosed in an intricately worked box. The success of the project derives from its superb execution, which, in this case, was carried out not by German construction workers, but by Swiss cabinetmakers. They have achieved a perfect grid of materials, with, for example, alternate elements offset horizontally by a very small amount at the ends of walls, imparting a minute sense of movement to this serene environment. Even the design of supports for the handrails was carefully considered, with a hand-friendly oval section supported on oxidized bronze.

'Switzerland suggests a certain connection with nature and also the precise character associated with its people,' Bassam has said, referring to photographic research of old Swiss chalets with all-wood interiors. But whereas those chalets showed off traditional, but relatively rough, craftsmanship, his Berlin store is so smooth and finely finished that you want to stroke its walls. The timber throughout is European oak, used as boards with a section of 10 × 125 cm (4 × 61 inches) on the walls and floors. Bassam has used slats on the ceilings, and boards with black rubber insets on the stairs.

He has added only two elements to this harmonious interior. Shoes are displayed on simple white-lacquered cubes that sit on rubber feet. Intended to be used for a museum-style display, these cubes can be moved around the store easily, with their changing configuration generating changes of atmosphere. The other element is the furniture. Stools, benches, stacked storage trays and even hangers are all solid walnut. Red-lacquer trays in the cupboards add the only touch of colour. The stools, adapted from a Swiss tractor seat, were carved in the Bally factory in Switzerland, using the same technology as shoe lasts.

Bassam also used oak for a roof extension to the Bally headquarters building in Switzerland, and rolled out ideas from the German store to other key locations. In 2003, a new top management team was installed at Bally, who will doubtless introduce new ideas. As stores increasingly become places of entertainment, Bassam's approach looks even more restrained and tasteful, while reflecting the Zeitgeist of shop-as-museum. Swiss craftsmanship makes products that are built to last and, just as few Bally customers would discard their purchases at the end of one season, Bassam's store design should be allowed to enjoy the longevity to which it is suited.

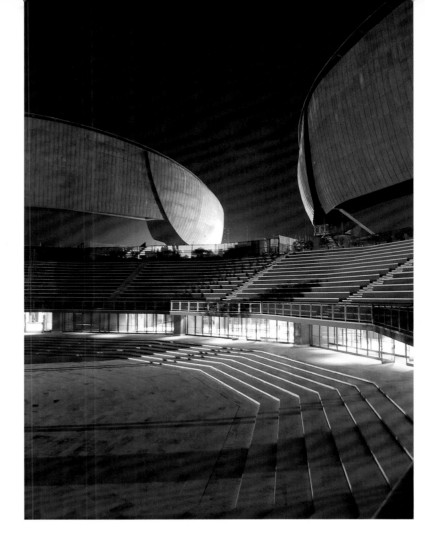

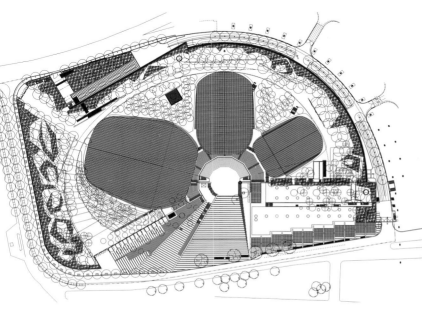

A contender for the title of the world's greatest living architect, Renzo Piano is a lover of materials. He received the first Spirit of Nature Wood Award, an international prize administered from Finland, for his work with timber, of which the most prominent example is the Tjibaou Cultural Centre, in Noumea, New Caledonia. It is one of the best-known yet least visited of contemporary buildings, because of its remote position. Far more accessible to most people is Piano's Parco della Musica in Rome. This building, fulfilling a long-felt need, is not, externally, a celebration of wood. The three linked concert halls are in brick, topped by wonderfully expressive bulbous lead roofs, albeit lined in pine and supported on arched glulam beams.

But if you reach the concert halls themselves, you will find yourself surrounded by timber, used in a sensuous and – given the precision of today's acoustic design – immensely practical manner.

Piano's masterstroke in the design of the Parco della Musica was not to try to shoehorn all the functions into one massive structure, but to put each of the three concert halls, of different sizes and functions, into a separate building. This makes sense both architecturally and acoustically. The three are linked and define between them a fourth space, an amphitheatre for open-air performances. This strategy paid dividends when, unsurprisingly for such

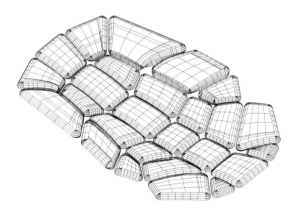

an archaeologically rich city, the site turned out to be perched on the ruins of a sixth-century Roman villa, which then had to be incorporated in the complex – a much simpler task with an agglomeration of buildings than with a monolith. As described by Piano, 'In our project the three halls, each set in a container resembling a giant sound box, were arranged symmetrically around an empty space, which became the fourth auditorium, not included in the initial programme: an open-air amphitheatre. Amid these constructions, luxuriant vegetation established a connection with the nearby park of Villa Glori.'

Each hall has a different function and, as well as being designed to give optimum quality for live performances, offers high-quality recording opportunities. Acoustic consultant Helmut Muller went through a lengthy process to ensure that the acoustics were right. First, he built models with reflective surfaces and used lasers to trace the route followed by reflections. From this he created diagrams of acoustic response, and fed the data into a computer to simulate the reflections of the soundwaves. The final stage entailed analogical tests – that is, using real sound – on large-scale models.

The smallest hall, with a capacity of 700, is intended for concert operas, baroque and chamber music, and theatrical plays. Based on some of the

solutions that Piano first used at the IRCAM experimental music centre in Paris 20 years ago, the space is extremely flexible, with movable walls and floors. This flexibility makes it possible for the hall to host symphonic performances, for which the stage arch opens up and thereby redefines the layout of the stage.

The 1,200-seat hall is also flexible in terms both of acoustics and layout, with a movable stage and an adjustable ceiling. It has space for a large orchestra and choir, but can also be used for ballet and contemporary music.

The largest hall, with 2,756 seats, is for symphony concerts with large orchestras and choir. It is about the largest feasible size for a concert hall – any bigger and there would be unacceptable reflections from the back. As well as straightforward acoustic considerations, audiences tend to feel uncomfortable in a larger space. The hall is of the vineyard type, meaning that the audience is divided into small, asymmetric rising blocks of steps. The vertical surfaces of the divisions create early lateral reflections into all sections of the audience. The best-known representative of the type is still Scharoun's Berlin Philharmonie, completed in 1963. At Parco della Musica, the orchestra is placed midway between the centre and the rear of the hall, with some seating behind it.

THIS PAGE
TOP LEFT   A total of 26 curved caissons form the roof of the large symphony hall.
ABOVE   In the symphony hall, some of the audience is seated behind the orchestra.

OPPOSITE
TOP   The vineyard design, used in the symphony hall, places the audience in small, asymmetric groups at different levels.
BOTTOM   Using cherry for the caissons gives a wonderfully warm feeling to the symphony hall.

OVERLEAF
However good the design, a performance space never reaches its full potential until it is filled with people.

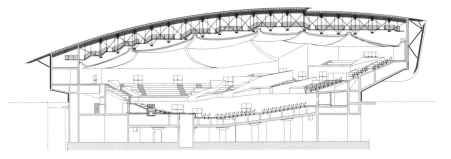

OPPOSITE
The medium-sized hall seats 1,200. It has an adjustable ceiling and a movable stage for maximum flexibility of use.

THIS PAGE
Seating 700, the smallest hall is intended for more experimental works.

The timber used for all the hall interiors is American cherry. A rich and warm-looking timber, with colour variations that add depth to its appearance, it also performs superbly acoustically. Many acoustic designers, especially in more northerly latitudes, favour larch for concert-hall interiors, but, although it can be beautiful, it lacks the sensuality of cherry. At Parco della Musica, the cherry is most dramatic in appearance in the largest hall, where it is used in the 26 curved caissons that descend from the ceiling.

Even such matters as the choice of fire retardants needed to be considered carefully. Piano commissioned test panels from manufacturers, and

eventually selected a retardant known as Saverlack, on the basis of its transparency and its adhesion.

The combination of its complex local politics, funding problems and over-abundance of archaeological riches means that Rome has taken a long time to achieve the musical centre it needs. But Piano's solution was well worth the wait. And despite the centre's use of the most up-to-date technology and bold contemporary architectural forms, it is an eminently comfortable setting for the music of the last three centuries – not least because of the use of timber and its association with traditional musical instruments.

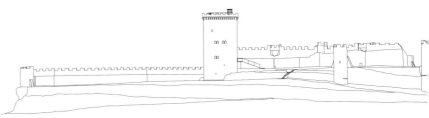

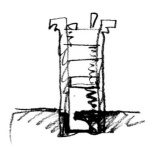

OPPOSITE

TOP   The castle at Peñaranda is in a commanding position, set on a ridge above the town.

LEFT   The design makes maximum use of views outwards.

RIGHT   There is a clear distinction between the new, timber interventions and the existing stone fabric.

THIS PAGE

TOP   The architect saw the tower as 'a hollow tube of stone emerging from the rocks' and designed accordingly.

ABOVE   The first of many stairs lead visitors to the entrance.

RIGHT   The simple square form and the crenellations on top give the tower a satisfyingly story-book aspect.

Castile, in northern Spain, is scarcely short of castles, but the castle at Peñaranda is one of the most dramatically sited. Peñaranda, 92 km (57 miles) from Burgos, is on the River Duero, which formed an important border in the long battles between the Moors and the Christians. The castle is set on a ridge above the town, with its battlements running dramatically along the contour. Most prominent of all is the Torre del Homenaje, a square tower with satisfying crenellations, looking exactly as a castle tower should look.

Although magnificent from the outside, the castle had lost its roof and internal floors. The city council stabilized and restored the structure, and then decided that its best use would be as a combined visitor centre and viewing point. In keeping with the best of heritage thinking, the council did not wish to make an irreversible intervention and therefore commissioned architects Carazo, Grijalba & Ruiz to design an internal structure that was, as far as possible, self-supporting.

The architects designed a timber structure, described as 'like a piece of furniture', which guides visitors up through the tower on eight levels. The architects saw the tower as resembling 'a hollow tube of stone emerging from the rocks', and wanted to maintain that impression. They felt that they could do this more successfully by suspending the

new structure from a few key points, rather than by supporting it from the ground. All the staircases, except the last one, consist of a single timber flight. Only at the very top do visitors use a small spiral staircase, contained within a glass enclosure, just visible like a periscope above the battlements.

The timber platforms are constructed of 18 x 40 cm (7 x 16 inch) laminated wood boards, with an oiled-oak top surface on birch ply. These boards are supported on sawed wooden joists, 8 x 16 cm (3 x 5 inches) in section. The steps of the stairs have been created from old railway sleepers, treated with creosote. Climbing all those stairs could be dispiriting, but the architect has ensured that at every level the experience is different. Making use of the few existing openings in the original structure, it has positioned windows on some of the platforms. Elsewhere, the visitor is both drawn on and intrigued by oiled-oak slatted screens, which both define the path and offer views. And the view from the top is magnificent, making it all worthwhile. Peñaranda has found an excellent use for its dominating tower, which should prove highly popular. But if the city decides one day that this use is no longer appropriate or desirable, it will be able to remove the architect's clever intervention without damaging the structure of a monument that has already stood for centuries and should remain for centuries to come.

OFFICE FOR LUNDBECK PHARMACEUTICALS
Milton Keynes, England | Artillery Architecture & Interior Design | 2001

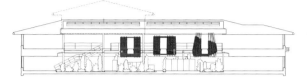

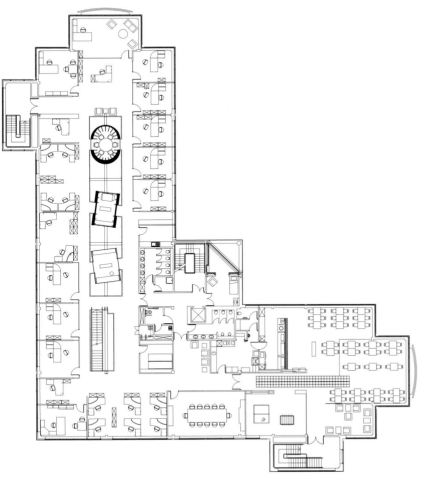

New ways of working in offices may have been pioneered by the 'creative' industries, but, by the end of the 1990s, the realization that communication was as important as doing mechanical tasks was spreading more widely. This is reflected in the UK headquarters of Danish company Lundbeck Pharmaceuticals, created by Artillery Architecture. The office is in Milton Keynes, a somewhat soulless town, but with good communications. Lundbeck took space in one of a number of mundane, speculative red-brick buildings on a business park, but was open to Artillery's relatively radical proposals for creating a home for its 67 employees. Offices are on two floors, and the architect cut a hole in the centre to create an atrium that acts as a hub, surrounded by working spaces. Natural light from the rooflight comes right down into the heart of the building.

Artillery treated the ground floor as a 'garden', a recreational space with plenty of plants, and with informal meeting spaces within it, plus some functional areas housing office equipment and storage. But the most dramatic intervention is at upper level, where the architect has created three 'pavilions'. Each a different shape — a cube, a trapezoid and an oval — they are all structurally the same. A steel framework is fixed to beams crossing the space, but there are glulam uprights and horizontal plywood cladding. The height of the cladding varies at different points on the perimeter, and there are spaces between the individual elements, so that occupants can see out, although from a distance the pods will be relatively opaque. The pavilions are used for informal meetings, to house a reference library and for photocopying equipment. Beams and cladding extend beneath the floors of the pavilions, so that the view from below is intriguing. Overall, the effect is of contemporary basketwork writ large.

Sales teams and their support services are the major users of this building, which means that many of them are only present infrequently. It was therefore thought important to make it a pleasant place for them to work, and one where they could catch up with information and office gossip. Other facilities include a gym, a canteen and a games room, but none is as visually distinctive as the three pavilions. As well as being a clever way of providing some facilities within what could otherwise be the dead space of the upper level of the atrium, the pavilions give out an important signal about Lundbeck. It is clearly a company that has thought about the working environment of its staff and is open to new ideas — both of which should help with recruitment in an increasingly competitive market.

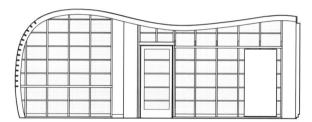

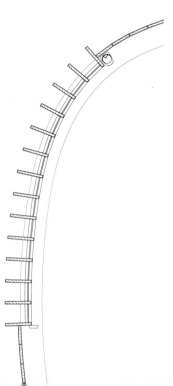

Advertising agencies often have the most playful of office buildings. Working their staff very hard, but with an ethos that work should be 'fun', and needing to impress their clients with their imagination and visual pizzazz, agencies can end up with offices that are not far removed from playpens. In those terms, Marmol Radziner & Associates' offices for TBWA\Chiat\Day in San Francisco could be seen as a positive paragon of sobriety. There are no primary colours, and there is a connection with the building's own history. But the architects have created an environment that is unusual without being wilful, playful without being perverse, and curvaceous without being disorientating.

Housed in an old brick warehouse, across the street from the headquarters of new client Levi Strauss, the office's design makes reference to the hulks of ships that were once abandoned there by those optimists taking part in the Gold Rush. It has exposed and exploited the great solid structure of the warehouse, while making insertions that set up a dynamic tension with the rectilinear grid.

Floorplates are cut away to create a double-height space that holds meeting rooms with sinuous profiles, clad in Douglas fir planks. In places, this cladding is solid, in others it is spaced to allow light to enter through polycarbonate glazing, also used on the ends of

the pods. By making all the cladding horizontal, the architect has strengthened the analogy with ships, although, in places, it is deliberately applied very loosely in a manner that is certainly not shipshape – more reminiscent of some rough-hewn crates. Inside the pods, the tightly planked and curved timber ceilings convey a feeling of captains' cabins in old sailing ships.

Workstations are ranged around the walls on the upper two levels, and there a sterner geometric is applied, with their enclosure in square forms reminiscent of crates, albeit rather refined ones. Made of apple plywood, they have wheatboard tops. Rice-paper lanterns

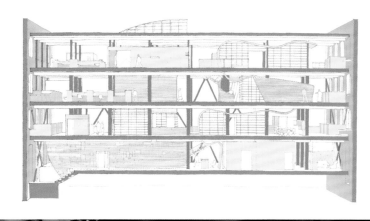

OPPOSITE

TOP LEFT The waiting area introduces a splash of colour.

TOP RIGHT Section through the old warehouse building, showing the architect's insertions. Areas that require isolation, such as the editing suites, are confined to the basement.

BOTTOM View of the first floor.

THIS PAGE

LEFT First- and second-floor plans, showing meeting areas in the centre, and workstations around the edge.

BELOW Workstations have square enclosures, made from apple plywood.

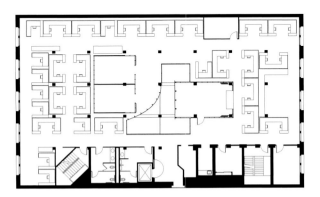

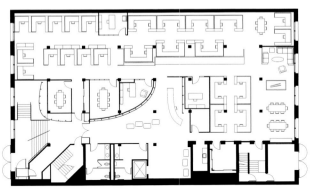

above the workstations provide a far less formal effect than does conventional task lighting. Other sturdy, but well-made, timber furniture looks as if it too would be at home on a high-class ship.

The floor in the reception area is of cork, but elsewhere is of Douglas fir ply. The odd touch of bright colour, as in the red soft furnishings and carpet of the waiting area, prevents there being an unrelieved brown palette.

Cleverly, the architect has banished those functions, such as editing suites, that require true isolation to the basement, creating out of the rest of the space a sense of community and communication, but with some privacy attached.

Chiat\Day has a history of commissioning imaginative buildings, from architects including Frank Gehry and Rem Koolhaas. If its San Francisco office is more restrained than some of its previous efforts, then it reflects the fact that advertising itself has grown up. Marmol Radziner has created an environment where it should be possible to work hard and to have fun, without the relentless pressure to be jolly and zany that some of the more wacky advertising offices impose, and which could, ultimately, be both wearying and depressing.

Timber is a solid, reliable material that will perform well if you don't ask too much of it; it cannot be used to achieve terrifically long spans and, compared with more modern materials, it is likely to be rather chunky. Such an assessment is right only up to a point. These were the known attributes of timber in the days when using it in construction meant cutting down trees of variable properties, doing a bit of seasoning and knocking up a building within the restrictions that this imposed. But, even in the Middle Ages, designers were using their ingenuity to achieve longer spans in halls and churches. Now — with engineered timber solutions, computer-based calculations and a knowledge of how to enhance the behaviour of timber by using it in conjunction with other materials — there is almost nothing that cannot be achieved.

Nearly every project in this book demonstrates the new understanding that architects and engineers have of timber and of the uses to which it can be put. What distinguishes the projects in this chapter is that the design teams responsible for them have taken that understanding to an extreme, achieving something that may previously have been considered impossible. And what they have done is clear for all to see. These are buildings likely to prompt even the casual observer to say, 'I didn't know you could do that with wood.'

At the Bodegas Vina Perez Cruz in Chile, José Cruz Ovalle has used glulam, a material that has become almost common currency, in one of the most exciting and sensual ways possible (see page 174). The curves he achieves, the imaginative use of spaces that in the hands of a less-talented architect would otherwise be wasted, and the timber interior that gives one the impression of being inside a wine barrel, are combined with a profound understanding of the building's intended purpose.

Flitched timbers — timber elements combined with steel plates — have a longer pedigree than glulam, since their development was not dependent on the introduction of modern adhesive technology. But, again, exploitation of their potential has advanced rapidly in the last few years, and in the enclosure for the Greenport Carousel in New York, Sharples Holden Pasquarelli have taken this to a new level, using an exceptionally hard timber that, in combination with other steel elements, allowed the members to be more slender than might previously have been thought possible (see page 196).

Shigeru Ban also used steel elements in combination with timber in his design of the Atsushi Imai memorial gymnasium (see page 180). Ban is an architect whose work is dedicated almost entirely to achieving things not

previously thought possible. Fascinated by the lightweight and by minimizing the use of materials, he has used laminated strand lumber to create a dome that not only spans 28 metres (92 feet), but also has to support heavy snow loads.

Concrete is used in conjunction with timber at the timber-engineering school in Biel-Bienne, Switzerland, where architect Meili & Peter set out to challenge preconceptions about timber buildings (see page 190). The school's four-storey building, with large windows, looks too big and too open either to function structurally or to satisfy fire requirements. Partly by concealing a stabilizing timber structure, and partly through the use of a concrete spine, the architect found a way around both these problems to create a building that adds to the ways timber can be used.

If the Biel-Bienne building is likely to be emulated more for its technical solutions than for its appearance, so, in a very different way, is Shin Takamatsu's Myokenzan worship hall in Japan (see page 184). This is such a bravura building — doing extraordinary things not only with timber, but also with steel and glass — that there is unlikely to be a place in the world for any imitators. But the astonishing nature of the achievement should prove to doubters that the potential for materials, and particularly for timber, is virtually limitless.

BODEGAS VIÑA PEREZ CRUZ

Paine, Chile | José Cruz Ovalle | 2001

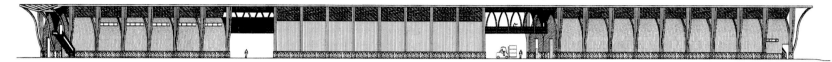

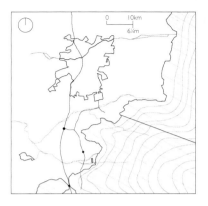

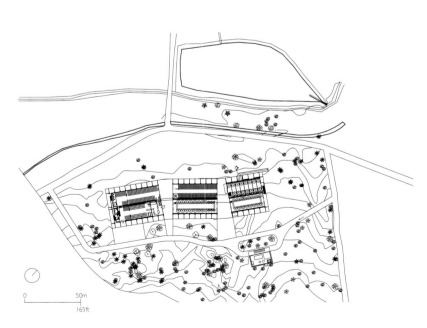

Chile's wine industry is growing fast, and the Maipo valley, only about 50 km (30 miles) from Santiago, has ideal growing conditions. Its quasi-Mediterranean climate includes many days without rain. But families such as the Perez Cruz, who have planted grapes on 530 hectares (1,310 acres), see their estates simply as working places. They have not developed the culture of day trips and longer tourist visits that lies behind the design of such extraordinary structures as Bodegas Ysios in Spain, designed by Santiago Calatrava (see page 126).

This makes it all the more remarkable that the Perez Cruz have commissioned a truly extraordinary building to serve what are, effectively, purely industrial purposes. The design, by expatriate Catalan José Cruz Ovalle, is sensuous and expressive – he has a secondary career as a sculptor – yet fulfils all the specific needs of wine production and storage. Above all, it is a magnificent expression of the use of wood. Apart from some concrete columns and walls of stone infill used up to shoulder height, it is an undiluted celebration of the material. Externally, sinuously curved glulam columns support the overhanging roof. Internally, the impression is of the kind of coopering technology used to create the barrels that, to a winemaker, are second in importance only to the grapes. The

material used is radiata pine, the main plantation timber in Chile. Although in the past the material has been seen as of relatively poor quality, this is changing as plantations become better managed.

The roof unifies three buildings that run roughly from southwest to northeast, but with a change in direction of about 15° between each to allow the buildings to follow the topography. Intended as a sign of respect for the land, this also reduces the mass and formality of the structure, so that the pairs of curved glulam beams do not march along a single line, diminishing to a vanishing point, but curve in plan in a manner reminiscent of their curves in the vertical plane. Informal covered courtyards, created between each pair of buildings, can be used for delivery of grapes or collection of bottles. At other times, they serve as informal shady spaces for relaxation.

The oversailing roof, which slopes up gently from the centreline of the building complex, has a visible gridded timber structure on its underside. This grid tightens up at the openings between the buildings in response to the greater spans required. Seen from either of its long sides, the complex is dominated by the view of the roof overhang and the glulam beams. The extraordinary structure that the roof protects is only really evident from the

THIS PAGE
The glulam beams that support the roof curve
sensuously.

OPPOSITE
Concrete columns and walls of stone infill come up
to shoulder height; above that, everything is timber.

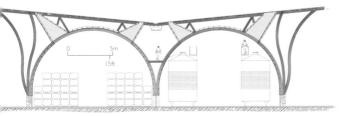

OPPOSITE

TOP LEFT — At the ends of the 'hidden passages', set between the tops of the two arches, there are views out.

TOP RIGHT — The form of the passages is determined by the curves of the arches, and by the clerestory glazing.

BOTTOM — A cellar, used for secondary fermentation, is also a dramatic space.

THIS PAGE

TOP LEFT — Section through the complex, showing the twin arched forms under a common roof.

ABOVE — The clerestory glazing brings a magical quality of light to the timber-lined spaces.

TOP RIGHT — Fermentation vats are a reminder that, however beautiful it may be, this is very much a working building.

other ends. Each building consists of two barrel-arched forms, running side by side. Entirely of wood, these are clad in relatively small timber elements. The consideration given to this cladding is symptomatic of the care that has gone into the whole design. Whereas the arching cladding runs directly along the curves of the arches, at the ends the cladding runs at 45° to the vertical, rather than simply vertically or horizontally. This is a much more lively experience for the eye, drawing it up and across the surface.

The functions of the buildings are arranged logically, with the entire eastern building and half of the central one dedicated to fermentation. The other half of the central building is for barrel storage. In the western building are the bottling plant, an area for bottle storage and an area for receiving materials. In some places there is a single space within the vault, in others there is a mezzanine floor. There is also a cellar beneath part of the building complex, used for secondary fermentation. With temperature control crucial, and also a requirement for some natural light, there is a clerestory on both sides at about the point where the walls would meet the roof, if this were not a continuously curved structure. Used primarily for ventilation, the clerestory also allows light to filter down into the building, imparting a wonderful glow to

the timber interior, as well as exposing the curved glulam beams at the top of the structure.

The point at which two barrel-vaulted structures meet is potentially awkward or, at best, a waste of space. But here the architect has made his most brilliant move. He has put in a floor, turning this into a continuous corridor of almost hexagonal shape. The lower two 'diagonals' curve, being the outer sides of the barrel vaults. Sometimes these open up to allow inspection of production processes. Between the buildings there are open views into the courtyard. Laminated timber elements are here in a range of sizes, sometimes solid and sometimes with gaps, unified by their colour. It resembles a showcase of the material in all its variety, while also giving the enticing impression of being in a secret place, in the sort of corridor that is sometimes created from the lost space beneath a castle's walls.

Despite being fiercely utilitarian, the Bodegas Vina Perez Cruz also has a magical quality, tempting the observer to speak in the superlatives that too often appear on winetasting notes. Winemaking may, after all, be an industrial process, but it is also one that has a special mystique and magic — and it deserves a building to match.

ATSUSHI IMAI MEMORIAL GYMNASIUM

Odate, Japan │ Shigeru Ban │ 2002

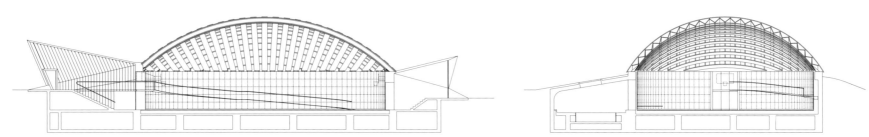

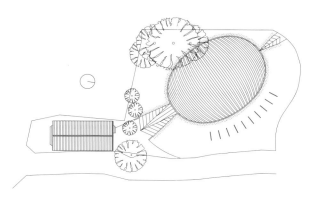

Japanese architect Shigeru Ban loves to experiment with technology, particularly with concepts of lightness, and is probably best known for his experiments in using cardboard as a structural material, most notably in the Millennium Dome in London and at Expo 2000 in Hanover. So, at first sight, he might not seem the obvious choice to design a structure in a place subject to notoriously heavy snow loads – a condition that normally calls for a very heavy structure to provide support. But Ban is an architect who embraces a challenge, and his design for the Atsushi Imai memorial gymnasium at Odate, in the north of Japan, is an indication of what can be achieved by a combination of imagination and rigorous analysis. Faced with having to construct a dome measuring 20 x 28 metres (66 x 92 feet), as the most efficient way to cover the gymnasium, Ban chose to use laminated strand lumber (LSL), a lightweight material and not one that would appear particularly suitable for dealing with snow loads.

The gymnasium is attached to a hospital, at which Ban had already built a smaller structure, a children's day-care centre, also using lightweight timber elements. But that building, although both innovative and beautiful, was considerably smaller and used laminated veneer lumber (LVL), in combination with a stabilizing steel outer frame. In the gymnasium, Ban was far more dependent on the timber itself to fulfil the structural requirements.

There is a very different precedent for the use of timber in Odate: a much larger dome designed by Toyo Ito, which uses massive cedar elements, in combination with steel trusses – a solution that Ban would shun both for the wastefully large volume of materials used and because it contravenes all his aesthetic concerns. Ban looked briefly at creating a moulded dome in LVL, but the material was not technically suitable. Moving on to the concept of using arches, he had to discover a way to make the structure strong enough to support snow loads. He chose LSL, a material similar to LVL but incorporating lower-grade logs, such as aspen, that are unsuitable for conventional timber products. Crucially, it is possible to make LSL in lengths of up to 28 metres (92 feet) and widths of up to 2.5 metres (8⅓ feet).

Ban's solution was to create a lattice of Vierendeel arches parallel to the longer axis, crossed by trussed arches parallel to the shorter axis. 'Just as paper could surprisingly be a structural member depending on how it is used, thin plywood can also be a structural element, which spans a distance beyond expectations,' Ban explains. 'With this solution, much less wood is used than

in an ordinary dome structure using other wood lamination.'

The trussed arches consist of LSL chord members and steel diagonal members. Since it is impossible to shape LSL 60 mm (2⅖ inches) thick into a curve, the material was divided into three lamina, each 20 mm (⅘ inch) thick. These were curved individually and then relaminated. The Vierendeel truss, which uses elements at right angles for stiffening, with no diagonal bracing members, consists of steel-pipe horizontal members, steel vertical members and LSL shear panels. The plywood is left entirely exposed internally, and the zigzag connections create a fascinating three-dimensional effect. The timber echoes the colour of the sports floor.

A circular concrete ring beam forms the base of the structure. Since surrounding buildings are low, Ban has set his building deep into the ground, so that it is already semi-submerged before being affected by snow. Only the dome itself and the two entrances are above ground level. The dome is clad with translucent polycarbonate that has

strips of stainless steel lying above it. This combination allows a considerable amount of light into the gymnasium, giving it an appealing sense of connection with the outside world. A swimming pool, set to one side of the dome, is entirely underground, and also benefits from strips of light penetrating its roof.

Ban was more confident in his innovation than the structural engineers with whom he worked, who persuaded him to incorporate more steel elements than he believed were necessary, either before or after construction. Nevertheless, the elements of the building were subjected to a very severe testing regime, with the behaviour of every component rigorously examined. As an architect who develops his ideas from one project to the next, Ban is likely to continue flying ever more freely from the constraints of conservative engineering. Having shown just what can be done with the cardboard tube, he is now demonstrating that, even under the most demanding technical conditions, timber can be used as a lightweight material in a manner more commonly associated with steel.

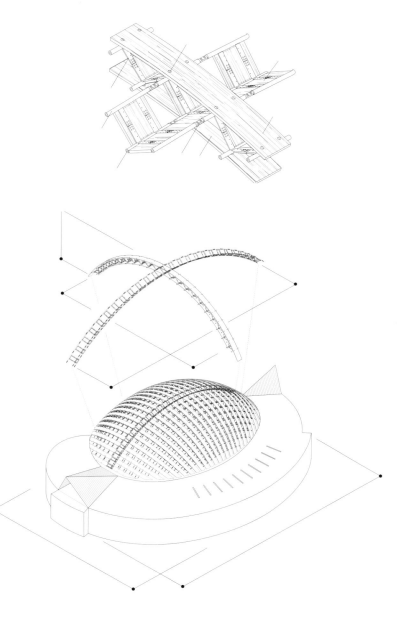

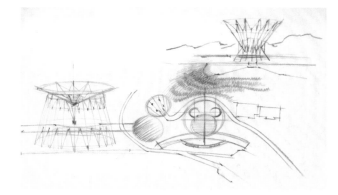

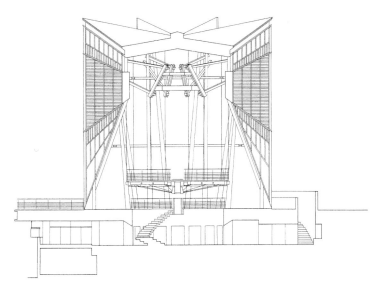

TOP Although known as an iconoclastic architect, Shin Takamatsu responded to the special nature of the building's setting.

BOTTOM The worship hall is set amongst a dense forest of cedars, with traditional Japanese buildings nearby.

THIS PAGE

ABOVE Both the geometry and the materials change as one travels up the building.

RIGHT Locally harvested cedar was used on the worship hall.

An extrovert complexity characterizes the work of Shin Takamatsu, an architect with many admirers and many detractors. Often colliding with the modern world and contemporary culture, he does not seem the obvious person to design a Buddhist place of worship. But this is exactly what he did at the Myokenzan worship hall, working for the first time with timber.

There is no established iconography for Buddhist places of worship, so Takamatsu had more freedom and a more open brief than if he had been designing a church or a mosque. What he did have was an important site, a place of great beauty, where the Buddhist holy man Myoken Bosatsu used to come to worship. Set in a wood of dense cedars, the worship hall is near a group of traditional Japanese buildings. Takamatsu himself has said about the building and about the use of timber, 'It is reasonable to hope that wood might provide some new way of deciphering beauty and structuring our culture; viz. by "structuring our mind". Since ancient times, Japan has used wood to construct the foundations of our "mind". People usually say that wood ought to be used on the spot where it is cut. This very simple way of thinking also applies to the "structure of the mind". The timber, which was harvested locally, is cedar, so the constructed form stands amid the natural material. But nobody could

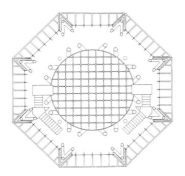

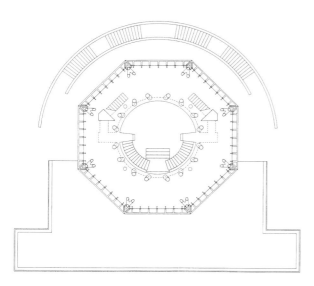

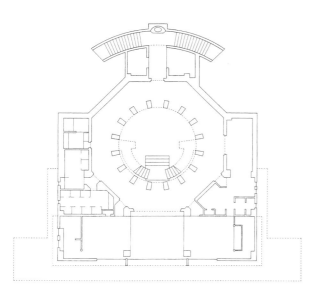

OPPOSITE
At night, with light shining out, the building looks like a magnificent mutant crystal.

THIS PAGE
LEFT   Plans showing (from the bottom) the first basement, ground floor and second floor give a sense of the changing geometry.
ABOVE   Transparent at ground level and at the top, the building has an opaque mid-section of cedar cladding.

mistake this for a 'natural' building, or for one that in any way evolved from its surroundings. Instead, it is a bravura tour de force, a symmetrical structure with a number of superimposed symmetries.

It has soaring form, whose plan transmutes from a circle to an octagon to an eight-pointed star. The materials change as one moves upwards, from concrete below ground level to steel to timber, and finally to a top level of glass, with an all-glass floor that allows the visitor to look down and be dazzled by the extraordinary geometry. The construction is not a simple layering of one material above another. Rather, the angular steel structure comes up from the circular concrete of the

underground structure to frame the prayer hall itself, and from within the prayer hall the timber structure rises up, clad externally in horizontal timber slats, a near-solid layer sandwiched between the filigree glazing above and below. Impressive enough in the daytime, the building is stunning at night, when light shines out of a form that seems like some kind of mutant crystal.

Buddhism is a famously non-prescriptive religion, so there is no one to dictate what the thoughts should be of those inside the worship hall. But it is a good bet that they will include at least a measure of amazement and awe at the achievement, both imaginative and structural, of this remarkable building.

SWISS ENGINEERING & TECHNICAL SCHOOL FOR THE WOOD INDUSTRY

Biel-Bienne, Switzerland | Meili & Peter | 1999

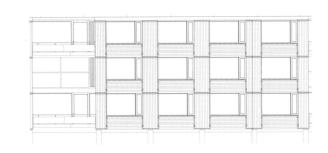

OPPOSITE

TOP The building is made up of 'cells' of prefabricated elements.

BOTTOM Planed, untreated oak cladding is angled to ensure that rainwater runs off.

THIS PAGE

RIGHT The size and form of the building distinguish it from its more traditional neighbours.

BELOW Spaces between the structurally independent timber boxes are used for balconies.

Assumptions about what a timber building should be, how it behaves and what is possible in timber construction have been turned on their head at a timber-engineering school in Switzerland. Architect Meili & Peter, appointed in competition to design the new teaching block, took the opportunity to challenge received ideas. It has succeeded in creating a building that is elegant and stern. Although, at first sight, the building hides its unconventional nature, its sheer scale and the size of the window openings are indications that something odd is going on – that this is, in fact, a revolutionary building. Almost every aspect is different from a traditional Swiss timber building. Aesthetically, there is none of the homely look of the conventional house, or indeed of the sheds that surround the new building. This is a more abstract architecture, concerned with defining spaces and bringing in light in a manner more usually attempted with the contemporary palette of steel and concrete.

At four storeys, the building was the tallest timber structure ever built in Switzerland, and there had to be considerable work done on the way that it would behave in fire. Other innovations include the extensive use of prefabrication, a floor design taken from first principles and an approach to acoustics that, although not entirely successful, provides some interesting

data. Given the identity of the client, it seems appropriate that the architect treated the building in some senses as a laboratory of ideas for timber construction. And, despite the fact that funding problems led to a gestation period of nearly ten years, the architect was sufficiently forward-thinking for its ideas to still seem radical when the building opened.

At 18 x 20 x 100 metres (59 x 66 x 328 feet), this is a substantial building. But it is not a single, continuous structure. Instead, it is made up of a series of self-supporting timber boxes, themselves built from storey-high prefabricated timber frames. The spaces between the boxes are used for circulation and to create balconies. Along the centreline of the building, where the main corridor runs, are four vertical concrete shafts, housing the lift, the staircases and the wc blocks. Each shaft is offset from its immediate neighbours to one side of the corridor or the other.

The corridor floors themselves are of heavily post-tensioned concrete. This concrete spine braces the building both longitudinally and transversely, and plays a key role in fire safety. Clad in steel, the corridors offer guaranteed escape routes. The balcony areas also act as fire havens. The spine does not extend the full length of the building. At the northwestern end, where a more

conventional, freestanding beam-and-post structure was adopted, are a library, lecture hall and exhibition space, occupying the full width of the building.

The rest of the building consists of five 'cells' made from prefabricated elements and capable of being divided into a varying number of classrooms. Six prefabricated timber wall elements, each measuring 2.7 x 9.7 metres (9 x 32 feet), make up a single storey of each cell. The floor/ceiling structure was also prefabricated. These floors, spanning between the walls, are hanging structures. The boxes are entirely independent, with no load transferring to the cores of the building. The fourth floor is a continuous structure, set behind a balcony. It holds together the 'cells' of the lower three floors. The roof, a timber structure supported on glulam beams, cantilevers above this upper storey. It is almost flat, draining down to the centreline of the building.

The palette of materials had a strong industrial influence: as-cast concrete, concrete floor screeds, steel and factory-finish timber. The use of solid panels provides the necessary stiffness to allow the large window openings. Façade elements, fixed from outside to allow replacement if necessary, are solid oak. The boards are simply planed and untreated, so quality control in their selection was crucial. Slightly inclined

THIS PAGE

TOP LEFT   The northwest façade has no openings, providing stability to the open structure that lies behind it.

ABOVE   The palette of materials is entirely contemporary.

OPPOSITE

LEFT   The top-level structure runs continuously from one end of the building to the other, helping to tie together the disparate elements lower down. Because it is relatively sheltered, cladding can be in less durable larch.

RIGHT   Cross sections through classrooms (top) and the foyer and exhibition space (bottom).

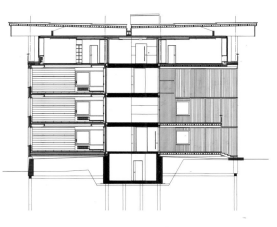

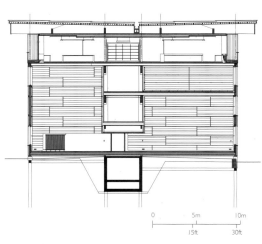

0   5m   10m

15ft   30ft

surfaces ensure that water will run off. The façade is ventilated, and panels are connected from the outside by special steel connections. There are no openings in the cladding on the northwest façade, providing further bracing to the open structure behind. Internal cladding throughout the building is of solid pine. Since the top floor is set back beneath the roof, and therefore receives considerable protection, it was possible to use larch, a less durable timber, for the cladding.

The timber floors formed the most complex element of the building because they had to deal with large loads and spans. In recognition of this, a separate competition was held for their design. The winning solution consists of a series of triple-cell elements, 32 cm (13 inches) high, spanning 8.5 metres (28 feet) as a single-span beam. These are made up of horizontal and vertical solid boards, joined by adhesives. To improve the acoustic performance, sections of the lower elements about 1.2 metres (4 feet) long were cut out to increase the sound-absorbing surfaces. However, this also had implications for fire safety, so calculations and full-scale tests were carried out to prove that the floor would still be able to provide 30 minutes' fire resistance.

To reduce the transmission of impact sound, it was necessary to increase the weight of the floor. In this case, a traditional method was used. First, 60 mm (2⅓ inches) of sand were laid on top of the floor structure. Above this went a floating particleboard floor, with a wearing surface above it of lightweight concrete. Between each trio of box elements there is a gap of 120 mm (5 inches), in which a sprinkler system was inserted – another part of the fire strategy.

A study produced at the school found that not all aspects of the building were entirely successful. Although acoustic isolation is good between floors and between the cells and the corridor, there is an unacceptable level of transmission between classes. The study notes that 'the floor system is considered as a rather expensive solution'. It also finds that the overhang of the roof does not provide as much solar protection to the top floor as was hoped, and that it can become very hot in summer. It is probably unavoidable that there should be some elements of failure in such an experimental building. What is equally important is that the school, which had undergone expansion and been upgraded to a university of applied science, has a building that both reflects its new role and demonstrates the possibilities of development in timber construction.

CAROUSEL HOUSE

New York, USA | ShoP/Sharples Holden Pasquarelli | 2001

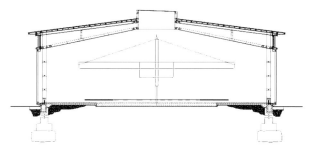

Old-fashioned carousels are romantic objects, evoking instant nostalgia, even in those people who have never seen one. So it is not surprising that the installation of an historic carousel in Mitchell Park, Greenport Village, on New York's Long Island, is playing a key role in the park's development. Built as a carnival ride in North Tonawanda, New York, in the 1920s, the 12 metre (40 foot) diameter carousel was donated to Greenport in 1995 by the Northrop-Grumman foundation. It is a traditional 'brass ring' carousel, with wooden horses and brass rings hanging from the edge, most of them tantalizingly out of reach. But fortunate or skilful children can grasp a ring at the height of their horseback journey and, even today, win a free ride.

The 1.4 hectare (4 acre) park is part of Governor George E. Pataki's programme to improve access to waterfronts across the state of New York. It links key elements in Greenport Village, including the ferry, Commercial Wharf, the main street and the marina. This former brownfield site is being given an identity by the New York architects SHoP/Sharples Holden Pasquarelli, working with the New York office of engineer Buro Happold. Key to the project is the use of timber, with a timber boardwalk linking important points, and the same timber used for shady arbours and the carousel house. This last item formed the major element of the first phase of the project.

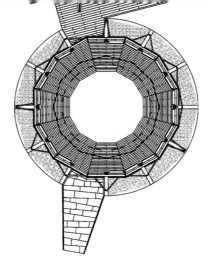

THIS PAGE
Site plan: the central 12-sided carousel house fits
well into the landscape strategy.

OPPOSITE
All the doors open (and can be closed, in case of
a storm) in less than 60 seconds.

Neither the carousel itself nor the public are as hardy as they used to be. It was therefore essential to provide shelter from the elements, but without either disguising the structure within a bland box or cutting off contact with the outside world, which is part of the pleasure of the ride on a fine day. The solution was a 12-sided timber enclosure that allows the carousel to be used all year round, responding to the changing weather with either partial or complete opening. In the worst weather, just one side opens partially. It echoes the form of the carousel and allows wonderful views, but is obviously a piece of advanced twenty-first-century engineering, rather than a romantic throwback. The effect is reminiscent of a beautifully constructed contemporary hatbox, enclosing a cherished old hat. It is an additional layer, both contrasting with and enhancing the charm of the original object.

Since the designers wanted the structure to be as slender as possible, they used flitched timber elements, which combine the best qualities of timber and steel in a composite, sandwich construction; the steel provides strength and stiffness, and the enclosing timber offers lateral stability, plus protection from fire and corrosion. Flitched beams are not a new form of construction – they were commonly used in industrial warehouses – but

newly available materials have made it possible to update techniques.

The carousel house uses high-strength steel plates, 1.9 cm (¾ inch) thick, sandwiched between ipe, an extremely hard and durable hardwood from Brazil that is naturally fire-resistant and resistant to rot. Flush-mounted stainless-steel hardware has also been used. The beams span about 8 metres (26 feet) from the exterior columns to a central compression ring that supports the stressed-skin plywood roof panels. The columns, constructed from double 10 × 30.5 cm (4 × 12 inch) ipe members, are spaced apart to provide slits of light between these deep members. The resulting increase in stiffness allowed the columns to be used as cantilevers, eliminating the need for cross bracing, which would have obstructed the doors. Shear key connectors were used at a number of locations to transfer the forces between the steel and timber members at the critical joints. These incorporated specially machined stainless-steel 'sex bolts' (the engineer's terminology), up to 30 cm (12 inches) long to pass through all members.

An independent system of structural steel members, propped off the main timber frame, supports the doors. These members house the worm-drive system that activates the doors. Each pair of doors is about 5 × 5 metres

(16 × 16 feet). The use of the worm drive allows the doors to be opened in winds of up to 64 kph (40 mph). Each door operates independently and can be opened or closed in less than 60 seconds. The engineers worked out the pattern of the doors by studying wave patterns common to both the movements of the carousel ride and its location on Peconic Bay. In this way, they provided both the greatest weather protection and the most atmospheric ride.

OPPOSITE
The Carter/Tucker
house, in Breamlea,
Australia, was the first
on which Sean Godsell
exploited the idea of
an outer cladding of
slats. The appearance
of the building changes
when flaps over the
door and various
windows are opened.

Not all buildings are immutable. Some have moving elements, and the appearance of others changes when seen from different angles, whether through reflection or obstruction of view. One of the most interesting ways in which this change can happen is through the use of timber screens and shutters.

As environmental awareness has increased, building designers in temperate zones have come to see the importance of shade – a quality long appreciated by the inhabitants of hotter countries. The brise-soleil – a horizontal metal grid, set above windows to keep out the hot summer sun – became a cliché of late-twentieth-century corporate buildings. Geographically, it was dominant in the region between the two zones where the wooden shutter is commonplace: the cold climates where the shutter provides insulation at night and the hot countries where loss of light is secondary to keeping out the heat.

Some contemporary architects have embraced the concept of the timber shutter, an object that may once have seemed irrevocably traditional. Aires Mateus, one of the most resolutely non-decorative of practices, has used shutters to animate the timber façade on its student accommodation in Coimbra, in Portugal (see page 222). The

appearance of the façade changes as individual students open and close their shutters. Herzog & de Meuron adapts an even more traditional-seeming element in its Paris apartment building (see page 208). It takes the technology of the rolltop desk and turns it into Oregon pine blinds for the informal courtyard façade of its building, giving residents both shade and privacy, while still allowing them to peep out.

If shutters are an integral part of much European architecture, then screens are similarly important in Japan. Kengo Kuma, who successfully blends the traditional with the contemporary, and feels a particular affinity with wood, makes excellent use of cedar slats in his Hiroshige Ando Museum (see page 218). The need for shade is only part of the story; the slats articulate a building with an almost simplistic design by providing a constantly changing pattern of light and shadow. Tadao Ando has created a shifting pattern of strips of light and shade with more substantial timber elements in his Buddhist temple on the island of Shikoku. He uses the elements for an outer, permeable wall, with interior circulation space.

Sean Godsell has taken a similar approach in Australia, with an outer casing of timber slats to his Peninsula House near Melbourne (see page 202). He takes advantage of the relative

abundance and extreme strength of the native jarrah timber to use it in slender and sharply detailed slats. The benefit of being able to see out, while being, at least partially, protected from prying eyes, is also a quality of an innovative old people's home near Paris, where the architect Maast has created a latticework of red cedar on the edge of a communal balcony (see page 214). This is part of a menu of timber, including wooden venetian blinds, that gives warmth to a building intended to be very much part of its local community, while still maintaining a distinctive identity.

Baumschlager and Eberle have married the sensation of changing patterns through timber slats with the 'moving parts' approach of blinds. The architects used this technique on a bank and office building in Wolfurt, Austria. Lattice screens slide back and forward, both changing the view of the building from outside and creating an enticing striped-light effect for those who choose to keep the screens across their windows.

All the effects described above are most likely to be enjoyed by those either inside the building or outside it, but relatively nearby. But changing patterns can also work on a larger scale. When Bucholz McEvoy designed Limerick County Hall in Ireland, it knew that part of its task was to create a new civic identity (see page 226). The brilliantly engineered timber screen on the main façade acts as a brise-soleil for the building's occupants, but is also designed on a large enough scale to provide a constantly changing and intriguing view for drivers on the nearby road. In this case, a device normally considered primarily as a way of maintaining privacy has mutated into a form of advertising. Who said that wood wasn't a versatile material?

PENINSULA HOUSE

Melbourne, Australia | Sean Godsell | 2002

THIS PAGE

ABOVE   The house is set into a hillside.

BELOW   Seen from above, the house appears to have
        burrowed into the landscape.

RIGHT   The jarrah cladding is very slender and beautifully
        detailed.

OPPOSITE
Glazing to the lower level of the sitting room can
open up completely.

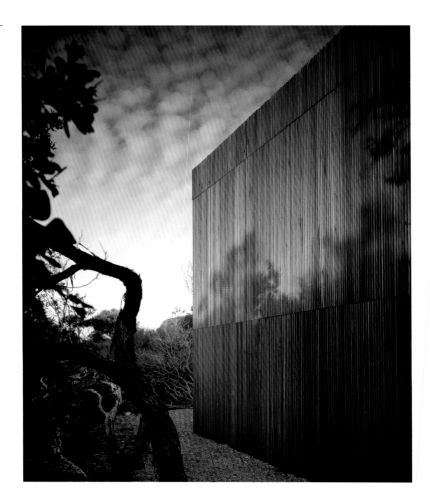

Jarrah is one of the densest and most durable of timbers. A native of south-western Australia, it has a high oil content that makes it resistant to insect attack. Melbourne architect Sean Godsell has used it to create a semi-transparent enclosure for a weekend house near his native city.

Put in the simplest terms, the house is a box within a box. The inner box is made of glass and pre-oxidized steel, the outer of recycled jarrah slats, fixed by galvanized steel elements to another oxidized steel frame. Staircases on either side, contained between the two frames, lead up to the carport and to the bedroom. Since jarrah is such a tough material, the slats can be very

slender – they are only 10 x 35 mm (⅖ x 1⅖ inches) in section. On the west side of the building, the secondary enclosure goes down to ground level; on the east side, it comes down to the top of the ground floor and then bends out at 90 degrees to shade a deck of radiata pine. There is a minimal south elevation, since the house is dug into a hillside. The northern façade is open, allowing sun worship and views of the sea.

Godsell has invented a clever way of shading his house from heat and glare. But the sharply defined slats do much more than that; they provide privacy and a changing appearance as one moves around the exterior. Seen straight on, they are relatively

ABOVE   Transitions between inside and outside are clearly defined, but not forbidding.

LEFT   The cladding angles out at 90 degrees to shade a deck of radiata pine.

OPPOSITE
Viewed straight on, the timber cladding is relatively transparent, but it becomes more opaque when seen from an angle.

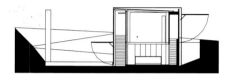

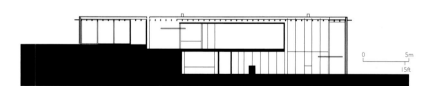

transparent, but become more opaque when viewed obliquely. For the house's inhabitants, they offer a pattern of shade that changes with the position of the sun, giving an indication of both the time of day and the time of year.

This second enclosure is impeccably detailed, subtly articulating the transition from ground floor to first floor, and from first floor to roof. Godsell has given similar care to the inner enclosure. The entire house is designed to give the inhabitants maximum pleasure in both the building itself and its surroundings. Visitors arrive at the upper level, at the carport on the south side of the building. From there, they go down the stairs to the double-height living room. This has fixed glazing on its upper half, but the lower half opens out entirely onto a veranda. Tucked back behind the living room are a kitchen and laundry with, behind them, a library. In contrast to the openness of the living room, this is a much more enclosed space, a pleasant retreat on a stormy day. The second staircase leads up to the bedroom, which cantilevers into part of the living space. Its end wall is also glazed, providing views out through the living room. Behind its bathroom, this bedroom has its own private courtyard, shaded by the jarrah slat roof.

This is not the first time that Godsell has used an enclosure of jarrah slats for a house by the sea. He first did it on the Carter/Tucker house, in Breamlea, Victoria, an even more enclosed-looking building that can open up in a number of intriguing ways (see page 200). Taking some of his ideas from the concept of the traditional Japanese house, Godsell has written that both these houses explore 'notions of inner room (*moya*) and enclosed veranda (*hisashi*). The main difference between the Carter/Tucker house and the Peninsula house is that, whereas the former treats the three main spaces similarly, in the latter the three primary spaces are very different in dimension, volume and quality of light.'

Godsell has received plaudits internationally for his beautifully considered work, but is less popular locally, where some decry his style and others his uncompromising criticism of much contemporary architecture. A tough, resilient substance such as jarrah seems an appropriate choice of material for this other native of south-western Australia.

APARTMENT BLOCKS

Paris, France | Herzog & de Meuron | 2001

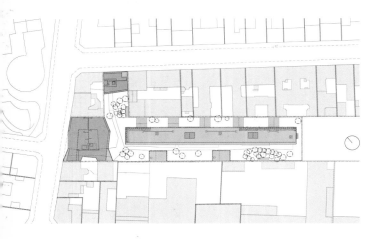

Anybody who has ever had access to a rolltop desk, especially as a child, will know the sensual, auditory and imaginative pleasure of opening and shutting the top – of making something solid curve away and disappear. Swiss architects Herzog & de Meuron have used this approach on a social housing development in the 14th arondissement of Paris, near the Gare de Montparnasse, creating sensuously curved timber shutters that use a rolling mechanism.

Named the Rue des Suisses after one of the streets onto which it faces – an appropriate name, given the provenance of the architects – the development was carried out for a forward-looking public-housing agency, Régie Immobilière de la Ville de Paris (RIVP). Building new social housing in the city centre was an admirable initiative since all but the wealthiest are increasingly being driven out to the soulless, and sometimes violent, areas that ring the city. By holding a competition and then appointing an internationally known and extremely innovative practice, RIVP was making a bold move, and one that paid off.

When the two founders of the practice, Jacques Herzog and Pierre de Meuron, won the Pritzker Prize, probably architecture's most prestigious award, in 2000, the jurors made the following comments: 'They refine the traditions

of modernism to elemental simplicity, while transforming materials and surfaces through the exploration of new treatments and techniques'; 'One of the most compelling aspects of work by Herzog and de Meuron is their capacity to astonish'; 'All of their work maintains throughout the stable qualities that have always been associated with the best Swiss architecture: conceptual precision, formal clarity, economy of means and pristine detailing and craftsmanship.' All these virtues were demonstrated in the Rue des Suisses project.

To the visitor, Paris is an immensely pleasing city – not only on account of its numerous architectural set-pieces, ranged mainly, but not exclusively, along the Seine, but also on account of the rhythm of its everyday buildings. Housing, typically between four and eight storeys high, with shops or other commercial activity at ground level, is rarely architecturally distinguished, although sometimes there are intriguing or imaginative details. More important are both the harmony of the individual buildings and the way they behave with each other, creating a coherent appearance that is not uniform enough to be dull.

This was part of what Herzog & de Meuron had to address, with two of its buildings breaking into the urban grid, on rue des Suisses and rue Jonquoy,

which runs at near right angles. Both these buildings have façades that match their neighbours in scale, although not at all in treatment. But this was not the whole of the commission. The project, which provides a total of 57 dwellings, includes not only the two seven-storey blocks with street frontages, but also a long three-storey block set within the city block, with no street frontage.

These backlands are another aspect of Paris, often not apparent to the visitor. Some blocks may be so small that they contain little more than a lightwell, but if you walk through certain neighbourhoods you quickly realize that the paucity of side streets means that the roads enclose an area much larger than could be accounted for by the footprint of the perimeter buildings. What is this area like? It is a much less ordered, formal world, sometimes described, confusingly, as a *cité*. Often closed off by a security gate, or just generally unwelcoming to the outsider, it typically contains a random assemblage of buildings that consitute a secret world. This is a place where, with little or no traffic, children can spill outside to play, a quiet world apart without the theatre of a city street – representing, in short, the introduction of an almost suburban way of life into the heart of the city.

Herzog & de Meuron have addressed this condition by introducing a three-

THIS PAGE

ABOVE LEFT — Small maisonettes are set opposite the three-storey block.

ABOVE — A sharp bend in the path that leads away from the block enhances the sense of privacy.

OPPOSITE

TOP — The plan is a series of 'T' shapes, enclosing private gardens behind for ground-floor residents.

BOTTOM — Exposed concrete at the ends of the block has wires on it, up which plants are being trained.

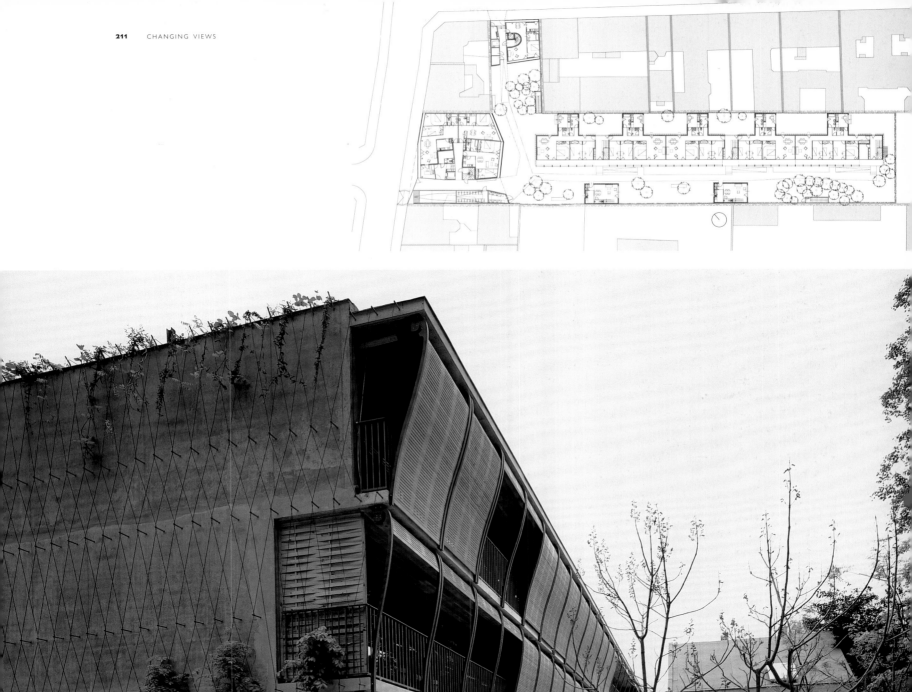

OPPOSITE
The timber shutters enclose spaces that are
generous enough to sit in.

THIS PAGE
RIGHT   With the shutters open, residents can supervise
children playing in the space below.
BELOW   Shutters have a different profile on each floor, but all
use the mechanism of the rolltop desk.

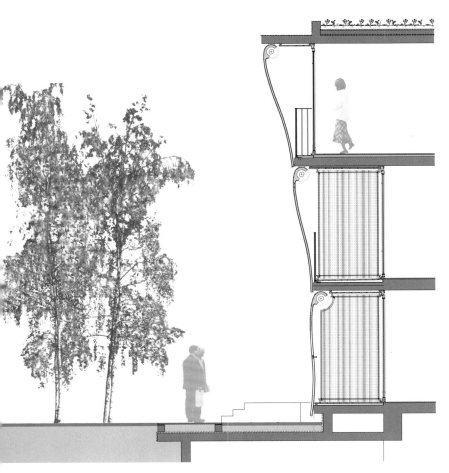

storey block that is both formal enough
to impose some rhythm on the site and
relaxed enough to reflect the virtues of
its more easygoing environment.
Entrances are on the long southern
façade, and it is here that the architect
has deployed the roller-shutter device.
Made of Oregon pine, on aluminium
guide rails, the shutters are used on all
three storeys. They cant out from a
dramatically overhanging roof on the
top floor, with a similar, though less
extreme, slope on the middle floor, and
follow an almost vertical line on the
ground floor, where they come down
to overlap the small, raised concrete
platform, on which the apartments have
been sited to keep them apart from the
public passageway. At all levels, the living
rooms and bedrooms are at the front,
with service spaces set behind.

On the ground and middle floors, there
are open terraces with floors of broad
timber planks behind the shutters,
whereas on the top floor there is simply
a small balcony railing in front of the
full-height sliding glazing. Set out with
garden furniture, these are places for

both relaxing and supervising children.
The architect has acknowledged that, at
this temperate latitude, there are times
when the sun is welcome and others
when it needs to be kept out. The
shutters serve to exclude the sun, as
well as providing privacy and security.

The ground-floor apartments are
T-shaped, enclosing small, private, north-
facing gardens at their rear. This is a truly
suburban touch for a city-centre site,
but the south façade, with its blend of
individual and communal relationships, is
more successful. It changes constantly, as
individuals alter the position of their
blinds – a facility also employed on the
street-facing blocks with perforated
aluminium shutters. The roller shutters
have their own natural perforation
between the slats, so that, even when
the shutters are closed, the occupants
of the apartments can gain some sense
of the exterior world. Herzog & de
Meuron have shown that its original
approach to materials and their
deployment can be made to work
within the restricted funds associated
with a social-housing project.

HOUSING FOR FRAIL ELDERLY PEOPLE (MAPAD)

Tremblay-en-France, France | Maast | 2002

OPPOSITE

TOP   Horizontal timber cladding is used widely
             throughout the project.

BOTTOM   There are private, enclosed spaces, with plenty of
             planting.

THIS PAGE

ABOVE   In contrast to the widespread use of timber, the
             reception building is distinguished as a stark
             white block.

RIGHT   Set on a triangular site, the development both
             engages with the outside world and provides some
             sheltered spaces for the disorientated.

France is carrying out a programme to replace conventional, asylum-like old people's homes with accommodation more suited to the needs of today's elderly people. New types of home are being built and evaluated; they vary according to the needs of the residents and the locations. Among these are MAPADS (maisons d'accueil pour personnes âgées dépendants), which are designed to house between 40 and 80 elderly people with physical or mental problems. One of the first to be built was at Tremblay-en-France, a small town near Paris's Roissy airport. Isabelle Manescau and François Marzelle of architect Maast won a competition to design the building on a triangle of land beside a main road.

Their challenge was to create a building that related visibly to the town and allowed residents to see their surroundings, yet would not seem hopelessly out of scale with the single-family homes and small blocks of flats among which it was set. They achieved this by dividing the project into a three-storey accommodation block and a large multi-use hall, linked by the reception, medical and administration building. With generous use of gardens and planting, plus the widespread use of wood for cladding, blinds and screens, they have created an environment that is domestic, without being twee, and which both engages with the town and offers places of refuge from it.

The accommodation building is set on a curve, following the line of the road, from which it is separated by rows of fruit trees. On its inner side are two gardens, one on either side of the reception building, with the more contained of the two dedicated to the use of those residents who are disoriented. Internal streets run along the garden side of the accommodation building, widening into seating areas that allow social interaction. This design places the bedrooms on the street side. Although, even with the barrier of trees, this will make the bedrooms less quiet than they would otherwise be, research shows that most residents of old people's homes and sheltered accommodation are eager to look out on everyday life and people. On the ground floor, each room opens onto a small enclosed garden. On the upper level, these gardens are replaced by a continuous balcony.

Rooms have walls clad in timber panels, with timber venetian blinds to the full-height windows that open onto the balcony. Externally as well, timber cladding is used – Navirex plywood panels on the outer façade and red cedar in a latticework effect on the courtyard side. This cladding is echoed on the hall, a large rectangular building whose different form does not stand out because of the similarity of external treatment.

The residents, some of whom may go out only infrequently, can look in one direction from their balconies and in the other direction from the seating area. By opening and closing the blinds, they change the look of the building's outer façade, bringing home clearly to the townspeople that this is an inhabited building and very much a part of their environment.

HIROSHIGE ANDO MUSEUM

Bato, Japan | Kengo Kuma | 2000

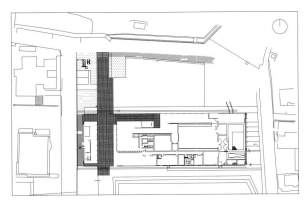

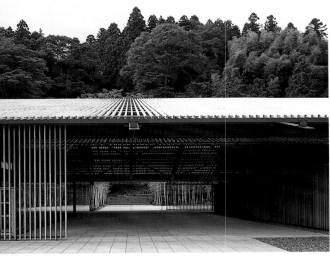

'Wood sits at the centre of Japanese culture. I use chopsticks every day,' said Kengo Kuma, when he won the second Spirit of Nature Wood Architecture Award in September 2002. 'My body feels uncomfortable in a concrete structure,' he added. 'I don't like the smell, I don't like the feeling of concrete.' He also talked about the importance of continuing to build with native Japanese cedar if the country's traditions are to be maintained. Although Japanese cedar is often more expensive than imported materials, only by continuing to use it will Japan be able to maintain and regenerate the forests that cover about 60 per cent of the landmass and are intricately bound up with the country's traditions and culture.

At the woodblock print museum in Bato, about an hour's drive north of Tokyo, Kuma has used local Yamizo cedar on the roof and to create screens. The museum houses the work of Hiroshige Ando, one of the country's most renowned artists, and the building might have turned out to be an exercise in traditional Japanese architecture. But when Kuma won the award, the judges cited the way 'he has successfully combined new and traditional elements to produce architecture that is completely modern while still being sensitively and carefully adjusted to its existing surroundings' – and the Bato museum is an excellent example of that. It is crisply engineered and uncompromising in a manner that brings

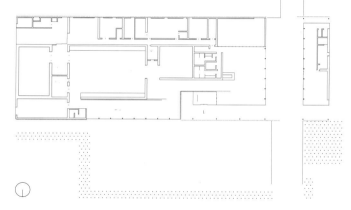

right up to date the traditions for which Kuma has shown so much respect.

Covering an area of 5,587 square metres (60,138 square feet), the building could not be simpler in its overall form: a single-storey rectangle, with some mundane elements tucked away in a basement. It has a shallow-pitched roof and, within its barn-like dimensions, contains two exhibition spaces, an open gallery and all the usual administrative and educational functions of a gallery. A public right of way runs through the western side of the gallery, and beyond this are a restaurant and shop.

The building has a simple steel frame. Its roof, made of six rows of cedar slats on each of the two slopes, rests above glazing, allowing the slats to cast shadows into the building. On the long, north side of the building, the most public aspect, there is a screen of cedar slats running almost the entire length, again in front of glass. This combination of timber slats and glass allows the timber to be seen from both inside and out. It also allows bright sunlight during the day and interior lighting at night to set up patterns of constantly changing reflections, which make it difficult to be sure what is structure and what is reflection, and to identify the boundary between inside and out.

There is no such confusion when one comes to the exhibition areas themselves. These are entirely enclosed, so that the lighting can be controlled. Gentle fibre-optics provide an acceptable degree of illumination for the delicate paper of Ando's prints. But the timber theme continues in suspended cedar ceilings, with dark voids behind them. Combined with the dark blue of the walls, this creates a sufficiently subdued environment to allow visitors to focus on the work.

Other materials used within the building are also local and traditional: Karasuyama *washi* handcrafted paper for the walls and dark Ashino-ishi stone for the floors. Kuma has described his concept of the museum as a place that 'expresses the artistry and tradition of Hiroshige by means of a traditional, yet subdued exterior'. A guide to the museum explains that, for those interested simply in the architecture, it is not necessary to visit the exhibition spaces. Indeed, despite the importance of Hiroshige Ando's work, there are likely to be many visitors who come simply to see how well Kengo Kuma has realized his concept.

THIS PAGE

TOP LEFT   The building contains two exhibition spaces, open gallery space and, to the far side of the public passage, a restaurant and shop.

TOP RIGHT Light coming through the layers of timber and glass has an almost tactile quality.

ABOVE   Exhibition spaces are entirely enclosed, to protect the delicate works on paper.

OPPOSITE

TOP   Traditional handmade paper, called *washi*, is used for the inner walls of the circulation areas.

BOTTOM   A simple steel frame supports the cedar cladding.

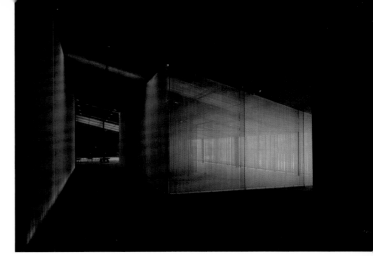

STUDENT HOUSING

Coimbra, Portugal │ Aires Mateus e Associados │ 1999

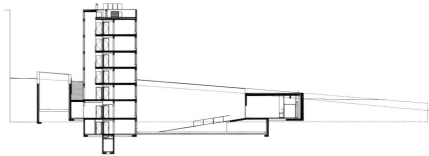

Founded in the thirteenth century, the University of Coimbra is the second oldest in Europe and still a dominant presence in this small Portuguese town, midway between Lisbon and Oporto. Its latest accommodation, squeezed onto a small triangular site, has been designed by Aires Mateus e Associados, a practice that has been described as 'Portugal's rising star'. Although the practice is more accustomed to working with concrete, in Coimbra it uses timber to animate one of the flush and severe façades that are becoming a trademark of the practice's work.

The complete lack of adornment on the façades somehow makes the window openings seem smaller, so that one is surprised to discover that there is, in fact, plenty of natural light inside. The architect has chosen to put most of the accommodation at one end of the site, where it rises to the maximum permitted level of eight storeys. This block runs north–south, with, at right angles to it, a two-storey accommodation building. A common room, tucked into the apex of the triangle, helps create a central, enclosed courtyard, into which the bedsitting rooms of the tall building face.

In total, there are 52 bedsitting rooms, with a toilet and shower shared by each pair of rooms. The rooms in the tall building face east, across the courtyard, while those on the southern block look

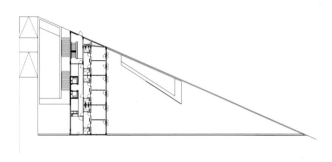

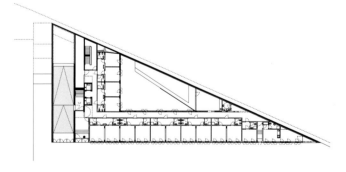

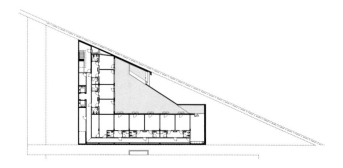

outward, to the south. It is these façades that are animated with timber.

At Coimbra, the architect has clad the façades in 8 mm (⅓ inch) phenolic-resin-bonded plywood in front of a ventilated cavity, insulation and blockwork. These are 80 cm (31 inches) wide, and come in three different heights. The window openings to the bedsitting rooms are the same height as a medium-height façade panel and are two panels wide. These windows have 20 mm (¾ inch) thick pivoting plywood shutters that the residents open and close as they wish. With windows on each floor slightly offset from those below, this creates an attractively randomized pattern. At night, if all residents choose

to shut out the light, the building closes down completely. This game with patterning is similar to one the practice used on a university building in Lisbon, although there the irregular patterning was permanent.

The timber façades contrast with the others, which are of exposed, white concrete blocks, with a rough surface that can reflect the sunlight. The only openings on the tall block on these façades are on the south-west corner, where horizontal slots allow light to penetrate into small common rooms. Otherwise, these are forbidding, if beautifully realized, faces that give no sign of the playfulness of the timber façade that lies around the corner.

LIMERICK COUNTY HALL

Limerick, Ireland | Bucholz McEvoy | 2003

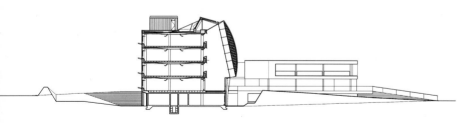

THIS PAGE

TOP   The *brise-soleil* shades the 75 metre (246 feet) long western façade of the office building, from which the council chamber juts out.

ABOVE LEFT   The façade is designed to make a good impression on motorists driving past.

ABOVE RIGHT   By canting the glazing and using the *brise-soleil*, the architect was able to give staff views of the constantly changing skies of western Ireland, without overheating the building-length atrium.

OPPOSITE

Vertical bowstring trusses, joined by timber members, make up the screen.

In a resurgence of municipal pride, numerous civic buildings have been constructed or planned in Ireland during the past decade. Designed by distinguished architects from within the country and from overseas, they tend to emphasize openness, communication and an environmental agenda.

Bucholz McEvoy made its mark when it won an open international competition in March 1996 to design the county hall for Fingal County Council in Dublin. Based in Dublin, the principals of the practice are US-trained Merritt Bucholz and Karen McEvoy, who, although trained in Dublin, has worked overseas with practices including Michael Graves

& Associates and Emilio Ambasz & Associates. The pair followed up the acclaimed Fingal building with the Limerick County Hall at Dooradoyle, which was the Irish entry at the 2002 Venice Biennale, while still under construction.

Although largely a concrete structure, Limerick County Hall has a delicately engineered timber *brise-soleil* along its long western façade that forms an integral part of the environmental strategy of the building, as well as creating its public face. For people driving past on a newly created road, the county hall provides a continuously changing face, a signal that this is a building of some importance, with

OPPOSITE
Timber elements joining the trusses are triangular in section, to ensure that they shed snow. Placing them close together increases shading and provides no space for pigeons to perch.

THIS PAGE

TOP RIGHT   Connections between the steel bottom chords of the trusses and the timber elements are in stainless steel, for durability.

BELOW   Considerable prototyping was needed in the evolution of the design.

enough glimpses inside to reflect the concept of 'open government'.

The siting of the building is unusual. It forms a gateway to semi-natural open space along the Ballynaclough River, but stands at the intersection of this open space and a large shopping centre, surrounded by a parking area. The offices for 260 council staff are contained within a north–south oriented rectangle, with an atrium running the full length of the western façade. This is intended to provide pedestrian links with both existing and future developments, and the architect has embraced the concept of the adjacent shopping mall to offer a similar level of accessibility within its building. Rather than being lost within this large building, the council chamber juts out at right angles from the western façade, so that the timber screen forms a backdrop to it.

At 75 metres (246 feet) long and 15 metres (49 feet) high, the timber screen was engineered by Paris-based RFR. Not merely an add-on, it forms an engineering whole with the canted glass wall behind it. The architect was keen that those inside the building should be able to enjoy the rapidly changing skies of the west of Ireland, and tipping the glazing made this possible. The screen itself consists of a number of vertical bowstring trusses, of which the lower chord is of galvanized steel and the catenary arch and all connecting members are of timber. The lower chords provide stiffening and anchorages for the glass wall.

Horizontal timber members join the trusses to each other, running from the bow of one to the bottom chord of the next. Combined with the cross members in the trusses themselves, which are more numerous than pure structural considerations would require, they provide shading from the sun when it is in all orientations from south to west. The members linking the trusses are triangular in profile, reflecting the fact that they have to support their own self-weight across a span of 3 metres (10 feet) and also deal with snow loads.

A variety of materials can be used for *brises-soleil*, and, given the widespread use of concrete in the rest of the structure, timber might not have seemed the obvious choice. But, as far as the architect was concerned, it was; it symbolized the green credentials of the building, provided a low embodied energy and helped to provide a link with the natural landscape. The building has a design life of 120 years, and the timber had therefore to be robust. It is an inherently tough material, but detailing, design and processes all had to be considered carefully to ensure that it did not suffer.

The timber is Scots pine (Pinus sylvestris) from the Czech Republic, which was shipped to Austria in 12 metre (39 foot) lengths for cutting into strips, gluing, forming and finishing. The common, although increasingly controversial, copper chrome arsenic (CCA) treatment for timber has been banned in Austria for a number of years, and instead a copper chrome boron (CCB) treatment was used. Establishing the correct gluing regime required some rather nerve-racking testing.

Gluing is an exact science, and there is an interaction between the preservative treatment and the glue. In glulam, the type of glue required changes with the laminate thickness. Whereas the requirements are well documented for timber that has had a CCA treatment, there is little information available for CCB-treated timber. The glulam contractor, Weihag, advised increasing the thickness of the laminate strips from 25 to 33 mm (1 to 1⅓ inches). It made up a sample and put this in a weathering oven. When the results turned out well, it adopted this strategy on the building. Another potential difficulty was the

connection between the timber and the galvanized steel chord. To isolate the two incompatible materials from each other, all fixings from the steel to the timber were done in stainless steel.

It was essential that water did not gather in any of the timber joints, so the sections were always designed with a sharp upper surface to ensure that water would fall away from the joints. Birds can be as much of a hazard as rain, since their droppings are not only unsightly, but also a source of chemical attack. The lateral members were spaced to ensure that they were too close together for pigeons to perch. On the top parts of the trusses, where this ploy would not work, anti-bird spikes were used.

Such attention to detail is unlikely to be noticed by the motorists speeding past, but they should certainly appreciate the interest of the façade. And, if they are driving some distance, they may be able to see how the building compares with others in Ireland's distinguished roster of civic offices.

APARTMENT BLOCKS
Rue des Suisses, Paris
CLIENT Régie Immobilière de la Ville de Paris
ARCHITECTS Herzog & de Meuron
PROJECT TEAM Béla Berec, Andrea Bernhard,
Christine Binswanger, Jacques Herzog,
Robert Hösl, Sacha Marchal, Mario Meier,
Pierre de Meuron
COMPETITION 1996 Herzog & de Meuron
PROJECT TEAM Béla Berec, Christine
Binswanger, Jacques Herzog, Susanne Kleinlein,
Mario Meier, Pierre de Meuron, Reto Oechslin,
Stephan Wolff
CONSTRUCTION SUPERVISION Cabinet
A.S. Mizrahi
GENERAL CONTRACTOR Bouygues SA

ATSUSHI IMAI MEMORIAL GYMNASIUM
Odate, Japan
PROJECT TEAM Shigeru Ban, Nobutaka Hiraga,
Soichiro Hiyoshi, Keita Sugai
STRUCTURAL ENGINEERS TIS & Partners –
Norihide Imagawa, Yuuki Ozawa
MECHANICAL ENGINEERING ES Associates
GENERAL CONTRACTORS Obayashi Gumi

BALLY STORE
Berlin, Germany
ARCHITECT Craig Bassam, Bassam Fellows
(formerly Craig Bassam Studio)
GENERAL CONTRACTOR Blumer Schreinerei
LIGHTING DESIGNER Dinnebier Licht Berlin

BODEGAS VIÑA PEREZ CRUZ
Chile
ARCHITECT José Cruz Ovalle
ASSOCIATE ARCHITECTS Hernán Cruz S,
Ana Turell S-C
COLLABORATOR M. Ramirez
STRUCTURAL ENGINEER R.G. Ingenieros y
Mario Wagner
TECHNICAL COORDINATION Ramón Goldsack

BODEGAS YSIOS
Laguardia, Spain
ARCHITECT Santiago Calatrava
ENGINEER Santiago Calatrava

BRENTWOOD SKYTRAIN STATION
Vancouver, Canada
CLIENT Rapid Transit Project Office
DESIGN TEAM Busby + Associates
ARCHITECTS B. Billingsley, M. Bonaventura,
P. Busby, S. Edwards, T. Mullock, M. Nielsen,
R. Peck, A. Slawinski
STRUCTURAL ENGINEER Fast & Epp Partners
MECHANICAL ENGINEER Klohn Crippen
ELECTRICAL ENGINEER Agra Simons
LANDSCAPE ARCHITECT Durante Kreuk
PUBLIC ARTIST Jill Anholt

CAROUSEL HOUSE
Greenport, New York, USA
CLIENT Village of Greenport, New York
ARCHITECTS SHoP/Sharples Holden Pasquarelli
STRUCTURAL ENGINEER Buro Happold
Mechanical Engineer: Laszlo Bodak Engineer, PC
ELECTRICAL ENGINEERS Leonard J Strandberg
& Associates/ Laszlo Bodak Engineer PC
CIVIL ENGINEER Leonard J Strandberg &
Associates
LANDSCAPE CONSULTANT Quennell
Rothschild & Partners, LLP
LIGHTING CONSULTANT Universe Lighting
GENERAL CONTRACTOR Carriage Hill
Associates, Inc.
ELECTRICAL CONTRACTOR Johnson Electric
Construction Corporation
DOOR FABRICATOR L. D. Flecken, Inc.
CARPENTER J.E. O'Donnell Construction
Co, Inc.

CHESA FUTURA APARTMENT BUILDING
St Moritz, Switzerland
CLIENT SISA Immobilien AG
ARCHITECTS Foster and Partners –
Norman Foster, Graham Phillips, Stefan Behling,
Matteo Fantoni, Sven Ollmann, Kate Carter,
Jooryung Kim, Judit Kimpian, Tillman Lenz,
Cristiana Paoletti, Stefan Robanus,
Carolin Schaal, Horacio Schmidt,
Thomas Spranger, Anna Sutor, Michele Tarroni,
Huw Whitehead, Francis Aish
Küchel Architects – Arnd Küchel, Vic Cajacob,
Martin Hauri, Georg Spachtholz,
Francesco Baldini, Thomas Henz,
Thomas Kaufmann, Richart Kevic
STRUCTURAL ENGINEERS Edy Toscano AG,
Ivo Diethelm GmbH, Arup
MECHANICAL & ELECTRICAL ENGINEERS
EN/ES/TE AG, R & B Engineering GmbH
ACOUSTIC ENGINEERS Edy Toscano AG
QUANTITY SURVEYOR Davis Langdon &
Everest
CLADDING CONSULTANT Emmer Pfenninger
Partner AG
LIGHTING Reflexion AG
CONCRETE O Christoffel AG
TIMBER STRUCTURE Holzbau Amann
GLASS LOBBIES Buehlmann AG
SHINGLES Patrick Staeger
ROOF Dachtechnik AG
WINDOWS HFF Fenster und Fassaden AG
COMPUTERS Siemens Switzerland
DOORS Lualdi
STONE Vogt
PLASTERBOARD Palombo
KITCHENS Bulthaup
TIMBER FLOORS Hagetra
METALWORK Pfister

CHILDREN'S LEISURE CENTRE
Chessy, France
CLIENT SAN du Val d'Europe, Ville de Chessy
ARCHITECTS Philippe Lankry Avant Travaux
Architects
ENGINEERING/CONTRACTOR Alto Ingénierie
SA
SHELL SPE
WOOD STRUCTURE Paris Charpentes
ROOFING Répisol
EXTERIOR JOINERY SHMI
INTERIOR JOINERY Fériaud
FLOORING EFI
PLUMBING SEED
ELECTRICS Thevenet
LIFT Kone

COUNTRY HOUSE
Granada, Spain
Eduardo y Luis Javier Martín Martín

DOWNLAND GRIDSHELL
Sussex, England
CLIENT Weald & Downland Open Air Museum
ARCHITECTS Edward Cullinan Architects –
Edward Cullinan, Robin Nicholson, John Romer,
PROJECT ARCHITECT Steve Johnson
STRUCTURAL ENGINEER Buro Happold –
Michael Dickson, Richard Harris, Chris Williams,
James Rowe, Oliver Kelly, Shane Dagger
SYSTEMS ENGINEER Buro Happold –
Doug King, Simon Wright
QUANTITY SURVEYORS Boxall Sayer –
Clive Sayer, David Foster, Paul Comins
PLANNING SUPERVISOR Boxall Sayer –
Clive Sayer
MAIN CONTRACTOR E.A. Chiverton –
Mike Wigmore, Chris Silverson
CARPENTERS The Green Oak Carpentry
Company – Andrew Holloway, Stephen Corbett
SCAFFOLDING Peri UK Ltd./Peri GmbH –
Howard Ball, Jurgen Kurth

EXPO CANOPY (EXPO-DACH)
Hanover, Germany
CLIENT Deutsche Messe AG
REPRESENTATIVE OF THE MANAGING BOARD
Sepp D. Heckmann
DIRECTOR FOR CENTRAL TECHNICAL OFFICE
Dr.-Ing. Rainar Herbertz
ARCHITECTS Herzog + Partner BDA –
Prof. Thomas Herzog, Hanns Jörg Schrade
PROJECT ARCHITECT Roland Schneider
Assistants: Jan Bunje, Peter Gotsch,
Moritz Korn, Thomas Rampp, Stefan Sinning
REALIZATION BKSP Projektpartner GmbH,
Hannover
PROJECT SUPERVISOR Ingo Brosch
Assistants: Wilfried Peters, Hans-Joachim Kaub
STRUCTURAL ENGINEERS IEZ Natterer GmbH.
Wiesenfelden – Prof. Julius Natterer, Dr.-Ing.
Norbert Burger, Assistants: Andreas Behnke,
Alan Müller, Johannes Natterer, Volker Schmidt;
Ingenieurbüro Bertsche, Prackenbach –
Peter Bertsche, Assistant: Peter Fitz;
Ingenieurbüro kgs, Hildesheim –
Prof. Dr.-Ing. Martin H. Kessel, Dirk Gnutzmann,
Assistants: Klaus Winkelmann, Georg Klauke
VIBRATION REPORT Technische Universität
München, Institut für Tragwerksbau –
Prof. Dr.-Ing. Heinrich Kreuzinger
PROOF ENGIENEERS FOR STRUCTURAL
ANALYSIS Ingenieurbüro Speich-Hinkes-
Lindemann, Hannover – Prof. Dr.-Ing. Martin
Speich, Dipl.-Ing. Josef Lindemann
COLOUR DESIGN Prof. Rainer Wittenborn,
München
LIGHTING DESIGN Ulrike Brandi Licht, Hamburg
PROJECT SUPERVISORS Marana Müller-Wiefel,
Oliver Ost
MEMBRANE PLANNING & ENGINEERING
IF Jörg Tritthart, Dr.-Ing. Hartmut Ayrle,
Reichenau/Konstanz, Engineers and architects
for lightweight structures
PROJECT MANAGEMENT Assmann Beraten
und Planen GmbH, Hamburg –
Dr.-Ing. Wolfgang Henning

SOIL REPORT Dr.-Ing. Maihorst & Partner,
Hannover
FIRE PROTECTION Hosser, Hass & Partner,
Braunschweig
FOUNDATIONS Renk Horstmann Renk,
Hannover
SURVEYING SERVICES Descoll v. Berckefeldt,
Hannover
EXTERNAL WORKS Dieter Kienast, Vogt Partner,
Zürich

HIROSHIGE ANDO MUSEUM
Bato, Japan
ARCHITECTS Kengo Kuma & Associates
COOPERATIVE ARCHITECTS Ando Architecture
Design Office
STRUCTURAL ENGINEERS Aoki Structural
Engineers
MECHANICAL ENGINEERS P.T. Morimura
& Associates
GENERAL CONTRACTORS Obayashi
corporation

**HOUNSLOW EAST UNDERGROUND
STATION**
London, England
CLIENT & PROJECT MANAGER London
Underground (Infraco JNP Limited)
ARCHITECT Acanthus Lawrence & Wrightson
QUANTITY SURVEYOR Dearle & Henderson
STRUCTURAL ENGINEER (roof &
superstructure) Buro Happold
CIVIL ENGINEER/M&E ENGINEER Infraco JNP
Limited
CLADDING CONSULTANT Buro Happold
CONTRACTOR Gleeson MC Limited
TIMBER FABRICATOR Cowleys Structural
Timber
STEEL FABRICATOR S H Structures
TIMBER TESTING University of Bath

HOUSE
San Prudencio Uleta, Vitoria, Spain
CLIENT Melquiades Pérez de Eulate
ARCHITECTS Roberto Ercilla and
Miguel Angel Campo

HOUSING AND STUDIOS
Newbern, Alabama, USA
Rural Studio, Auburn University

**HOUSING FOR FRAIL ELDERLY PEOPLE
(MAPAD)**
Tremblay-en-France, France
ARCHITECTS maast – François Marzelle and
Isabelle Manescau
CLIENT SAGE
ENGINEER GEC Ingénierie

LIMERICK COUNTY HALL
Ireland
ARCHITECT Bucholz McEvoy Architects, Dublin,
Ireland
CLIENT Limerick County Council
STRUCTURAL ENGINEER Michael Punch and
Partners
SERVICES ENGINEER Buro Happold
FAÇADE ENGINEER RFR Paris
QUANTITY SURVEYOR Boyd Creed Sweett
CONTRACTOR John Sisk and Co Ltd

MUNICIPAL SWIMMING POOL
Puentedeume, Spain
CLIENT Diputación Provincial de A Coruña
ARCHITECTS QRC architects – Antonio Raya,
Carlos Quintáns, Cristóbal Crespo
COLLABORATORS Santiago Sánchez, Enrique
Antelo, architects
CONSTRUCTION MANAGERS Antonio Raya,
Carlos Quintáns, Cristóbal Crespo, Diputación
de A Coruña Architectural Services – Marian
Juárez, Javier Fafián
CONTRACTOR Construcciones Mouzo y
Souto S.L.
MECHANICAL ENGINEERING INSELT, S.L.
CARPENTRY & WOOD Carpintería Hijos de
Romay, S.L.
AIR CONDITIONING ALTAIR, S.L.
ELECTRICITY ALTAIR, S.L.
WATER PURIFICATION AQUANOR, S.L.
STAINLESS STEELWORK Industrias Caamaño
S.L.
DAMPPROOFING Firestone Giscosa S.A.,
INSTALLATOR TRADISCO
PLUMBING Instalaciones RAYPA S.L.

MYOKENZAN WORSHIP HALL
Kawanishi, Japan
DESIGN TEAM Shin Takamatsu, Mitsuo Manno,
Masafumi Sato
STRUCTURAL ENGINEERS Toda Corporation
Structural Engineering Dept.
MECHANICAL ENGINEERS Architectural
Environmental Laboratory
GENERAL CONTRACTOR Toda Corporation

NUOVA FIERA EXHIBITION CENTRE
Rimini, Italy
CLIENT Ente Autonomo Fiera di Rimini,
Presidente Lorenzo Cagnoni
ARCHITECTS gmp – von Gerkan, Marg +
Partner
DESIGN Prof. Volkwin Marg
PROJECT MANAGER Stephanie Joebsch
TEAM Yasemin Erkan, Hauke Huusmann, Thomas
Dammann, Wolfgang Schmidt, Regine Glaser,
Helene van gen Hassend, Mariachiara Breda,
Susanne Bern, Carsten Plog, Marco Vivori,
Eduard Mijic, Arne Starke, Dieter Rösinger,
Olaf Bey, Uschi Köper, Beate Kling,
Elisabeth Menne, Dagmar Weber, Ina Hartig
LOCAL PARTNER ARCHITECT Dr. Clemens
Kusch
STRUCTURAL ENGINEERS Favero & Milan
CONSULTANTS Schlaich Bergermann und
Partner
TECHNICAL & ELECTRICAL ENGINEERS
Studio T.I.
CONSULTANT Uli Behr
LANDSCAPE DESIGN Studio Land, Milan

**OFFICE FOR LUNDBECK
PHARMACEUTICALS**
Milton Keynes, England
PROJECT CREDIT Artillery Architecture &
Interior Design

PAINTROCK CAMP
Hyattville, Wyoming, USA
ARCHITECT Charles Rose Architects Inc.
PRINCIPAL-IN-CHARGE Charles Rose
PROJECT TEAM Charles Rose, Eric Robinson,
David Gabriel, David Martin, Franco Ghiraldi,
Lori Sang, Takashi Yanai, Maryann Thompson,
Marios Christodoulides, Patricia Chen,
Heidi Beebe

PARCO DELLA MUSICA
Rome, Italy
CLIENT City of Rome
ARCHITECTS Renzo Piano Building Workshop
DESIGN TEAM, COMPETITION 1994 K. Fraser
(architect in charge), S. Ishida (senior partner)
with C. Hussey, J. Fujita and G.G. Bianchi, L. Lin,
M. Palmore, E. Piazze, A. Recagno, R. Sala,
C. Sapper, R.V. Truffelli (partner), L. Viti;
G. Langasco (CAD operator)
CONSULTANTS, COMPETITION 1994 Ove
Arup & Partners (structure and services);
Müller Bbm (acoustics); Davis Langdon &
Everest (cost control); F. Zagari, E. Trabella
(landscaping); Tecnocamere (fire prevention)
DESIGN TEAM, DESIGN DEVELOPMENT
1994–1998 S. Scarabicchi (partner in charge),
D. Hart (partner), M. Varratta with S. Ishida,
M. Carroll (senior partners) and M. Alvisi,
W. Boley, C. Brizzolara, F. Caccavale, A. Calafati,
G. Cohen, I. Cuppone, A. De Luca, M. Howard,
G. Giordano, E. Suarez-Lugo, S. Tagliacarne,
A. Valente, H. Yamaguchi; S. D'Atri, D. Guerrisi,
L. Massone, M. Ottonello, D. Simonetti (CAD
operators); D. Cavagna, S. Rossi (models)
CONSULTANTS, DESIGN DEVELOPMENT
1994–1998 Studio Vitone & Associati
(structure); Manens Intertecnica (services);
Müller Bbm (acoustics); T. Gatehouse,
Austin Italia (cost control); F. Zagari, E. Trabella
(landscaping); Tecnocons (fire prevention);
P.L. Cerri (graphic design)
DESIGN TEAM, CONSTRUCTION PHASE
1997–2002 S. Scarabicchi (partner in charge)
with M. Alvisi, D. Hart (partner) and P. Colonna,
E. Guazzone, A. Spiezia
CONSULTANTS, CONSTRUCTION PHASE
1997–2002 Studio Vitone & Associati
(structure); Manens Intertecnica (services);
Müller Bbm (acoustics); Techint/Drees &
Sommer (site supervision)

PARLIAMENT BUILDING
Karasjok, Norway
CLIENT Statsbygg
ARCHITECTS Stein Halvorsen AS Sivilarkitekter
MNAL and Christian A. Sundby Sivilarkitekter
MNAL

PENINSULA HOUSE
Melbourne, Australia
ARCHITECT Sean Godsell
PRINCIPAL Sean Godsell
PROJECT TEAM Sean Godsell, Hayley Franklin
STRUCTURAL ENGINEER Felicetti Pty Ltd
LANDSCAPE ARCHITECTS Sean Godsell with
Sam Cox
GENERAL CONTRACTOR Kane Constructions
(Vic) Pty Ltd

RAILWAY STATION
Aix-en-Provence, France
CONTRACTING AUTHORITIES RFF, SNCF
(Station Development Office)
DELEGATED CONTRACTORSHIP LN5 (SNCF)
PROJECT MANAGEMENT AND SITE
SUPERVISION Station Design Office (SNCF),
AREP
ARCHITECTS AREP – Jean-Marie Duthilleul,
Etienne Tricaud, Marcel Bajard, Eric Dussiot,
Gérard Planchenault (site manager)
LANDSCAPE ARCHITECT DPLG Desvigne
et Dalnoky
STRUCTURAL ENGINEER ARCORA
TECHNICAL ENGINEER Trouvin/BETEREM
GENERAL ENGINEERING COORDINATION
OTH
SCHEDULING, SITE MANAGEMENT
& PROGRAMMING COPIBAT

REEVE RESIDENCE
Lopez Island, Washington, USA
ARCHITECTS Cutler Anderson
PROJECT ARCHITECT Janet Longnecker
PROJECT DESIGNER Jim Cutler
PROJECT TEAM Julie Cripe, Bruce Anderson
CONTRACTOR Alford Homes (Lowell Alford)
MASON Tony Rothiger
STRUCTURAL ENGINEER Coffman Engineers –
Craig Lee, Deann Arnholtz
ROOFING CONSULTANT Ray Wetherhold

REMODELLING OF A HOUSE
Chamartín, Madrid, Spain
ARCHITECTS Nieto y Sobejano –
Fuensanta Nieto, Enrique Sobejano
COLLABORATORS Carlos Ballesteros,
Mauro Herrero, Juan Carlos Redondo
SITE SUPERVISION Fuensanta Nieto, Enrique
Sobejano, Arquitectos Miguel Mesas Izquierdo,
Aparejador
STRUCTURE N.B.35 S. L., Eduardo Gimeno
MECHANICAL ENGINEER Aguilera Ingenieros
S.A., Pedro Aguilera
MODELS Estudio Nieto-Sobejano

SCHOOL
Gelsenkirchen-Bismark, Germany
PROJECT MANAGERS Peter Hübner,
Martin Müller, Martin Busch
PROJECT TEAM FOR MAIN BUILDING
Peter Hübner, Filip Hübner (workshop);
Christoph Forster, Ulrike Engelhardt (studio);
Martin Müller (laboratory); Martin Busch
(pharmacy); Mathias Gulde (cinema);
Olaf Hübner (theatre); Thomas Strähle
(town hall); Peter Hübner, Reiner Wurst
(library); Peter Hübner (chapel); Olaf Hübner,
Akiko Shirota (bar and music); Thomas Strähle
(public meeting hall); Olaf Hübner (market
place); Bärbel Hübner (interior architecture);
Martin Busch (pyramid)

SHELTER
Campo de Vallemaggia, Switzerland
ARCHITECT Architect dipl. ETH Roberto
Briccola

STUDENT HOUSING
Campus II, Coimbra, Portugal
ARCHITECTS Manuel Aires Mateus, Francisco
Aires Mateus
COLABORATORS Henrique Rodrigues da Silva,
Filipe Nassauer Mónica, Gabriela Gonçalves,
Nuno Marques
STRUCTURAL ENGINEER Planear,
José Carvalheira
ELECTRIC ENGINEER Ruben Sobral
MECHANICAL ENGINEER Galvão Teles
PROJECT MANAGEMENT Rui Prata Ribeiro
CLIENT Serviços da Associação Social,
Universidade de Coimbra

**SWISS ENGINEERING AND TECHNICAL
SCHOOL FOR THE WOOD INDUSTRY**
Biel-Bienne, Switzerland
CLIENT Bau-, Verkehrs- und Energiedirektion
des Kantons Bern
ARCHITECTS Marcel Meili, Markus Peter
with Zeno Vogel
ARCHITECTS' COLLABORATORS
Andreas Schmidt and Thomas Schnabel,
Othmar Villiger, Thomas Kühne,
Urs Schönenberger (Project), Marc Loeliger
(Competition)
STRUCTURAL ENGINEER Jürg Conzett –
Conzett, Bronzini, Gartmann AG
STRUCTURAL ENGINEER'S COLLABORATORS
Reto Tobler (Concrete), Rolf Bachofner (Wood
construction)
ART Jean Pfaff
SITE MANAGEMENT Bauleitungsgemeinschaft
Hofmann + Huggler

SWISS PAVILION
Hanover Expo, Germany
Architect büro Peter Zumthor

TBWA\CHIAT\DAY
San Francisco
ARCHITECT Marmol Radziner and Associates
MANAGING PARTNER Leo Marmol, AIA
DESIGN PARTNER Ron Radziner, AIA
PROJECT MANAGER Anna Hill
PROJECT ARCHITECTS John Kim, Su Kim,
Brendan O'Grady
PROJECT TEAM Paul Benigno, Juli Brode, Patrick
McHugh, Chris McCullough, Daniel Monti,
Bobby Rees, Renee Wilson, Annette Wu
FURNITURE COORDINATOR Michael Holte

TOWER OF BABEL
Artists' Community of Ruigoord

VEGETAL BUILDINGS
Sanfte Strukturen – Marcel Kalberer, Bernadette
Mercx, Anna Kalberer, Peedy Evacic u.a

VIEW SILO HOUSE
Livingston, Montana, USA (Phase One – Silo)
CLIENT Ron Gompertz
ARCHITECTS RoTo Architects, Inc. –
Clark Stevens, AIA, Principal
COLLABORATORS Ben Ives, Dave Kitazaki,
Kirby Smith
TEAM Carrie DiFiore, Eric Meglassen
CONSULTANTS MT Structural –
John Schlegelmilch, Principal

VISITOR CENTRE
Peñaranda, Spain
ARCHITECTS Eduardo Carazo Lefort,
Julio Grijalba Bengoetxea, Victor J. Ruiz Mendez
PROJECT TEAM Detet Renner, Carlos Ruiz
QUANTITY SURVEYOR A. Grijalba Grijalba
CLIENT Ayuntamiento de Peñaranda de Duero
(Burgos)
CONTRACTOR Ortega S.A., Yofra (wood)

WILLOUGHBY DESIGN BARN
Weston, Missouri, USA
CLIENT Ann Willoughby, Willoughby Design
Group
DESIGN TEAM El Dorado, Inc.
PROJECT ARCHITECTS Dan Maginn (AIA),
Josh Shelton
STAFF Doug Hurt, Brady Neely, Chris Burk

Y HOUSE
Catskill Mountains, New York, USA
OWNER Herbert Liaunig
ARCHITECT Steven Holl Architects
PROJECT ARCHITECT Erik F. Langdalen
PROJECT TEAM Annette Goderbauer,
Brad Kelley, Justin Korhammer, Yoh Hanaoka,
Jennifer Lee, Chris McVoy
SITE ARCHITECT Peter Liaunig
STRUCTURAL ENGINEERS Robert Silman
Associates P.C.
LIGHTING CONSULTANT L'Observatoire
International
CONTRACTOR Dick Dougherty
CUSTOM MADE FURNITURE Face Design,
Chris Otterbein

PICTURE CREDITS

T = top
B = bottom
C = centre
L = left
R = right

6 Roderick Coyne
7T Temperate Forest Foundation/www.forestinfo.org
7B Forest & Wood Products R & D Corporation (FWPRDC)
8 Svenskt Limträ AB/ www.svensktlimtra.se
9T Guildhall Library, Corporation of London
9B Martine Hamilton Knight
10 Indav Oy, © Raute Oyj
11 Jussi Tiainen
12 Heini Schneebeli
13B Steve Mc Donagh
13T ©Dennis Gilbert/VIEW
14L Nic Le Houx
14TR Angelo Kaunat
15 Tim Soar
16 Studio ARP
17T Kirill Ovchinnikov, Vitalii Nefedov
17B © Jeremy Cockayne and Bernard Stilwell Architects
18 Jussi Tiainen
20 Marcel Kalberer
21TL Marcel Kalberer
21TR Philippe Rohner
22–23 Marcel Kalberer
24–27 © Friedrich Busam/architekturphoto
28–29 © Dennis Gilbert//VIEW
30 Edward Cullinan Architects Ltd
31–33 © Dennis Gilbert//VIEW
34–39 © Chuck Choi, Chuck Choi Architectural Photography
40–43 © Art Grice
44–49 ©Paul Warchol
50 © Carl-Viggo Hølmebakk
52–55 François-Xavier de Larminat photographe, Philippe Lankry
56–59 © Christian Richters
60–65 © Jaro Hollan
66–67 Eugeni Pons
68–69 Vicente del Amo
70–75 Nigel Young/© Foster and Partners
76 ©Timothy Hursley
78 © Peter Blundell Jones
79TL © Peter Blundell Jones
79TR Peter Hübner
80T © Peter Blundell Jones
80B Peter Hübner
81 Peter Hübner
82 © Peter Blundell Jones
83TL © Peter Blundell Jones
83TR&cr Peter Hübner
84–87 © Hollandse Hoogte
88–91 Cristóbal Crespo
92–95 Luis Asín, Hisao Suzuki
96–99 César San Milan
100–105 Mike Sinclair
106–111 ©Timothy Hursley
112 © Raf Makda/VIEW
114–117 Nic Lehoux
118–120 all images courtesy Buro Happold
118BL Acanthus, Lawrence & Wrightson
118TR Adam Wilson
119 Graham Young
120 Adam Wilson
122–125 RoTo Architects, Inc.
126–131 © Roland Halbe/artur
132 Michel Denancé
133TL Christian Michel
133TR Stéphan Lucas
134BL Didier Boy de la Tour
134TC Christian Michel
134TR Michel Denancé
135 Christian Michel
136 © D.Leistner/artur
137 Skyspan
139 © D.Leistner/artur
140–147 Klaus Frahm
148 Kirill Ovchinnikov, Vitalii Nefedov
150–153 © Paul Warchol Phtography, Inc.
154–161 Moreno Maggi, Enrico Cano
162–165 Luis Asín
166–167 Morley von Sternberg
168–171 © Benny Chan/Fotoworks
172 © Hiroyuki Hirai
174 Juan Purcell
175–179 © Roland Halbe/artur
180–183 © Hiroyuki Hirai
184–189 Toshiyuki Kobayashi
190–195 © Georg Aerni
196–199 © Karen Ludlam; plan and section: © ShoP/Sharples Holden Pasquarelli
200 Earl Carter
202–207 Earl Carter
208–213 © Margherita Spiluttini
214–217 Hervé Abbadie, François Marzelle
218–220 © Shinkenchiku-sha
221 Mitsumasa Fujitsuka/HELICO Co Ltd. Japan
222–225 © DMF
226–230 © Michael Moran, Michael Moran studios

AUTHOR'S ACKNOWLEDGEMENTS   I would like to thank the following for their help and encouragement in acquiring knowledge, making the book possible and bringing it together: Isabel Allen, Felicity Awdry, Philip Cooper, Susan Dawson, Helen Elias, Liz Faber, Paul Finch, Fredrika Lökholm, Sutherland Lyall, Hugh Pearman, Shelley Power, Catherine Slessor, Charles Trevor, Mark Vernon-Jones and, most of all, Barry Evans.